Osaka 1615

The last battle of the samurai

Campaign • 170

Osaka 1615

The last battle of the samurai

Stephen Turnbull • Illustrated by Richard Hook

First published in Great Britain in 2006 by Osprey Publishing,
Midland House, West Way, Botley, Oxford OX2 0PH, UK
443 Park Avenue South, New York, NY 10016, USA
E-mail: info@ospreypublishing.com

A CIP catalogue record for this book is available from the British Library

ISBN-10: 1-84176-960-6
ISBN-13: 978-1-84176-960-8

Page layout by The Black Spot
Typeset in Helvetica Neue and ITC New Baskerville
Index by Glyn Sutcliffe
Maps by The Map Studio
3D bird's-eye views by The Black Spot
Originated by United Graphics, Singapore
Printed in China through World Print Ltd

06 07 08 09 10   10 9 8 7 6 5 4 3 2 1

For a catalogue of all books published by Osprey Military and Aviation please
contact:

NORTH AMERICA
Osprey Direct, c/o Random House Distribution Center, 400 Hahn Road,
Westminster, MD 21157
E-mail: info@ospreydirect.com

ALL OTHER REGIONS
Osprey Direct UK, P.O. Box 140 Wellingborough, Northants, NN8 2FA, UK
E-mail: info@ospreydirect.co.uk

www.ospreypublishing.com

Author's dedication

To Oliver Brayshaw.

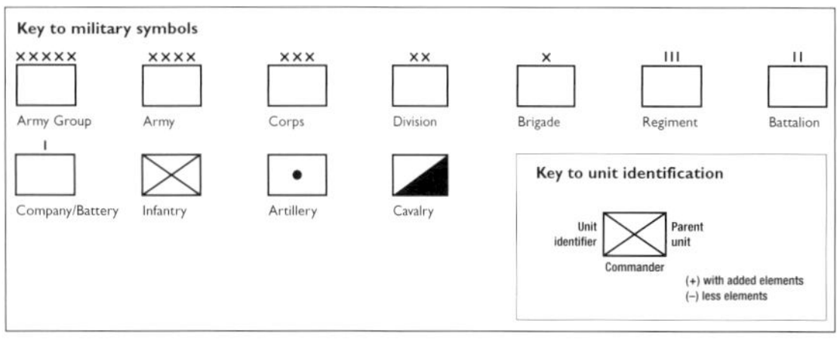

Key to military symbols

XXXXX	XXXX	XXX	XX	X	III	II
Army Group	Army	Corps	Division	Brigade	Regiment	Battalion

Company/Battery	Infantry	Artillery	Cavalry

Key to unit identification

Unit identifier — Parent unit — Commander
(+) with added elements
(−) less elements

Author's note

Following conventional Japanese usage, all names are given
with the family name first. Dates have been converted from
the lunar calendar to the Gregorian calendar using Bramsen's
Japanese Chronological Tables. As England had not adopted
the Gregorian calendar by the early 17th century, the dates
appearing on the letters of the East India Company have
been modified accordingly by adding ten days. For the further
convenience of the reader, the spelling in the quotations from
East India Company documents has also been modernized.
Dates of birth and death are given where known. All pictures
are from the author's own collection.

Artist's note

Readers may care to note that the original paintings from
which the colour plates in this book were prepared are
available for private sale. All reproduction copyright
whatsoever is retained by the Publishers. All enquiries
should be addressed to:

Scorpio Gallery, PO Box 475, Hailsham,
East Sussex BN27 2SL

The Publishers regret that they can enter into no
correspondence upon this matter.

Glossary of terms

daimyo	Japanese feudal lord
jokamachi	castle town
sakoku	the 'closed country' policy adopted by Japan in 1639
koku	measure of wealth expressed through the yield of rice fields
ninja	secret agent
ronin	samurai who has lost his master either by death or dispossession
samurai	member of Japan's military class
sashimono	identifying device, usually a flag, worn on the back of a suit of armour
seppuku	suicide by disembowelment, popularly known as *hara kiri*
shogun	the military dictator of Japan, a post created by Minamoto Yoritomo in 1192 (because of the term's familiarity in English it will appear here as Shogun)
shoshidai	the Tokugawa Shogun's Governor of Kyoto
yashiki	mansion

Weights and measures

The *tay*, a word used by the East India Company for the prices of goods, was
the anglicization of the trade name for the Chinese ounce (*tael*), equivalent to
$\frac{1}{16}$th of a *catty*. Although often reckoned at 6s 8d, the rate varied according to
the price of silver. The *tay* was therefore strictly a measure of weight, as was
one *pecul*, which was 100 *catties*, a weight of 60.6kg (133 ⅓lb) – this was often
used for measuring quantities of gunpowder. The usual figure given for the
contents of a barrel of gunpowder was 45.5kg (100lb), otherwise known as a
quintal, with the actual weight of the barrel making the total weight to at least
50.9kg (112lb). In the text, any references to *pecul* and barrel are roughly
equivalent. Japanese weights used for cannon refer to the weight of the shot
fired, i.e. using multiples of the *kanme*, a weight of 3.75kg (8 ¾lb), and the
monme, ¹⁄₁₀₀₀ th of a *kanme*.

CONTENTS

INTRODUCTION

The Osaka campaign – or rather campaigns, because it consisted of two distinct winter and summer operations – holds a unique place in Japanese history. The battle of Tennoji in 1615, with which the fighting at Osaka concluded, was to be the last occasion in which two armies of samurai would engage one another in a pitched battle. It also saw the final appearance on the field of war of Tokugawa Ieyasu, whose victory at Osaka secured his family's hegemony for the next two and a half centuries. But the Osaka campaign was also notable for a number of firsts. Because the fall of Osaka Castle was publicized by means of a woodblock-printed broadsheet, the campaign became the first event in Japanese history to be reported in anything resembling a newspaper. It was also the first major occurrence in Japan to be described in the English language – this was through the reports and letters prepared by the East India Company from its trading post in Japan. It was entirely appropriate that they should do so, because artillery supplied by the East India Company played a decisive role in the fall of the castle when it was used in the first long-range bombardment in Japanese history.

OPPOSITE **The outcome of the siege of Osaka Castle was reported in a broadsheet, thus making the siege the first event in Japanese history to be reported in anything resembling a newspaper. The scene shows the triumphant Tokugawa samurai pursuing defeated warriors and terrified townspeople, who plead for mercy. In the background the keep of Osaka Castle is shown on fire.**

ORIGINS OF THE CAMPAIGN

THE AGE OF WARRING STATES

The period of Japanese history between 1467 and 1615 is known by analogy with ancient China as the *Sengoku Jidai* ('Age of Warring States'). Throughout this time Japan suffered from sporadic civil wars between powerful *daimyo* (feudal lords), a long process that was finally brought to an end by the conflict at Osaka.

In their struggle for survival the rival warlords completely ignored both the nominal rule of Japan's sacred emperor and the supposed rule of the Shogun, or military dictator, a position created in 1192. The power of the Shoguns had declined rapidly during the Age of Warring States, and the post was temporarily abolished in 1568. From that year onwards, however, Japan had moved towards reunification under two particularly outstanding generals. The first to take steps in this direction was the brilliant Oda Nobunaga (1534–82), but he was killed in a surprise attack in 1582. The man who succeeded him was called Toyotomi Hideyoshi (1536–98). He was an accomplished general, and by 1591 Hideyoshi had conquered the whole of Japan. He then over reached himself with a disastrous war against China that was fought on the Korean peninsula. Hideyoshi died in 1598 in the manner that all dictators dread, because his son and heir Toyotomi Hideyori (1593–1615) was then only five years old. Very soon Japan split once again into armed camps. On one side was a loose coalition of *daimyo* who nominally supported Hideyori, while on the other were the supporters of his deadliest rival: Tokugawa Ieyasu (1542–1616).

Tokugawa Ieyasu was one of history's great survivors. Taken as a hostage when a child, and made to fight for one of Japan's least successful *daimyo* when a young man, he gradually asserted his independence and allied himself in turn with Nobunaga and Hideyoshi. His territory in eastern Japan, presented to him by a grateful Hideyoshi, allowed him to avoid service in Korea, and this ensured that his troops were in better shape than many of his rivals who had suffered in that conflict. By the summer of 1600 Ieyasu's potential was recognized by all, including the Portuguese traders, who had regular dealings with him and whose reports paint a vivid picture of the turmoil Japan was then experiencing.

Spain and Portugal had existed as a joint monarchy since 1580, a political unity that had enhanced the monopoly of Japanese trade that the two countries enjoyed between 1543 and 1600. Japanese arquebuses, copied from Portuguese originals brought in 1543 and then mass-produced, had made a considerable impact on the conduct of Japanese warfare. In 1600, however, Protestant rivals joined the Spanish and Portuguese when a Dutch ship visited Japan for the first time. The five vessels that made up the inaugural fleet left Rotterdam on 27 June 1598,

The keep and walls of Osaka Castle at sunset.

but only one made it to Japan, having become the first ship of any nation to do so via the Straits of Magellan. The vessel was the *Liefde*, which arrived off Bungo province in Kyosho, the main island of southern Japan, on 9 April 1600. To complete a trio of 'firsts', also on board the *Liefde* was the famous William Adams, the first Englishman ever to set foot in Japan.

The threat that this arrival posed to the existing Iberian trading hegemony became immediately apparent when the Portuguese insisted to anyone who would listen to them that the Land of the Rising Sun had just taken delivery of 'a party of piratical heretics'. This unflattering complaint was made very forcibly to Tokugawa Ieyasu, who is referred to by Adams as 'the great king of the land' – a prescient statement, for this was effectively what Lord Tokugawa was shortly to become.

As well as apprehending the crew, Ieyasu confiscated the armament of the *Liefde* for his own uses. The haul consisted of a score or so cannon, 500 arquebuses, 5,000 cannon balls, 50 *quintals* of gunpowder and 350 fire arrows, some of which may have been used at his decisive victory at Sekigahara on 21 October 1600. This huge battle destroyed the rival coalition, and three years later Tokugawa Ieyasu revived the post and title of Shogun. He made his own castle town, which lay 300 miles to the east, into Japan's new administrative capital. It was called Edo, and proved to be a highly successful choice, as may be judged from the fact that Edo is now known as Tokyo.

THE HEIR TO MISFORTUNE

Ieyasu's destruction at Sekigahara of the rival coalition of *daimyo* had one notable feature: the absence of any direct involvement in the name of Toyotomi Hideyori, the child whose inheritance lay at the root of the struggle. Ieyasu also made no hostile moves against Hideyori during the course of the Sekigahara campaign. Instead both Hideyori and his influential mother, Hideyoshi's widow Yodogimi, were successfully sidelined by political manoeuvres undertaken primarily by Katagiri Katsumoto, who had become Hideyori's personal guardian in 1599 following the death of Maeda Toshiie.

Katsumoto's efforts were rewarded by Ieyasu, who doubled his territories and moved him to a different province. The latter outcome was a phenomenon experienced by many other *daimyo* following the battle of Sekigahara, although it was not always a positive experience. They were shifted around Japan like pieces in a game of chess, with the size of their landholdings being either increased or decreased according to which side they had supported. These were the lucky ones. Others were either forced to shave their heads and become monks, or simply deprived of those heads by the swing of a samurai sword. Toyotomi Hideyori, forced into neutrality during the conflict, saw his revenues fixed at 657,400 *koku*, and was allowed to retain as his residence his late father's masterpiece of Osaka Castle.

Tokugawa Ieyasu's decision to make Edo into Japan's administrative capital did not mean that he had neglected to establish a firm power base for the Tokugawa family in the Kyoto/Osaka area. In fact the reverse was true, because not only did Ieyasu rebuild and strengthen Hideyoshi's Fushimi Castle to the south of Kyoto, where it controlled all

A statue of Tokugawa Ieyasu on the site of his castle of Okazaki. He is shown wearing the armour he wore at the battle of Nagakute in 1584, and is carrying his *maedate* (helmet badge).

Tokugawa Ieyasu at the battle of Sekigahara, shown in command within the *maku* (field curtain).

traffic towards Osaka, he also created a new castle in the heart of the imperial city itself. Nijo Castle, of which the surviving palace is today one of Kyoto's finest tourist attractions, was built very near to the imperial palace and became the base for the *Shoshidai*: the Tokugawa Shogun's Governor of Kyoto. His chief function was to keep close control of the activities of Japan's divine emperor and his court.

Edo, by contrast, became the focal point for controlling the *daimyo*. Many of them had already experienced considerable disruption to their lives by being moved to distant provinces. In the years following Ieyasu's triumph they had to suffer the further humiliation of being invited, then requested, and finally forced to send their wives and children to live in Edo under the protection of the benevolent Shogun. By the time of the third Tokugawa Shogun this glorified hostage system was to become the most successful means of social control that the Tokugawa were to exercise. In 1603 the process was just beginning, but the experience of Toyotomi Hideyori had already given several clues as to how it would develop.

In addition to confining Hideyori inside Osaka Castle, Ieyasu had entangled him within the bonds of matrimony. Marriage between *daimyo* families had long been regarded as a vital tool of social engineering. Ieyasu was no exception to this view, and had used marriage to cement a union between his family and the house of Toyotomi. Ieyasu's last consort had been Hideyoshi's sister. His son Hidetada, the second Tokugawa Shogun, was married to a sister of Yodogimi, and in 1603, at the age of ten, Hideyori was married to Hidetada's daughter. This meant that the Osaka campaign became a war between Toyotomi Hideyori and the man who was at the same time his uncle, his great-uncle and his grandfather-in-law.

Yodogimi, unsurprisingly, had not taken kindly to the disinheriting of her son Hideyori by this opportunist from Edo, but it was 1605 before she gave vent to her feelings in public. In that year Ieyasu retired from the post of Shogun in favour of his son Hidetada. Great celebrations were held, and Hideyori was invited to join in the festivities. Yodogimi, who was very suspicious of Ieyasu's motives, refused to let him leave Osaka. An anecdote tells us that she stated that she and her 13-year-old son would rather disembowel themselves than leave the safety of the mighty fortress. In certain accounts this comment is attributed to the year 1611, which was to be the only year in which Hideyori was successfully prised from his mother's grasp.

The meeting between Ieyasu and Hideyori in 1611 proved to be a memorable encounter. Prior to the event, Ieyasu took great pains to assure the Toyotomi family of his peaceful intentions, to the extent of placing two of his own sons – Yoshinao aged 12 and the nine-year-old Yorinobu – into the care of two trustworthy *daimyo* as token hostages. The interview with Hideyori was held at Nijo Castle and lasted two hours, and it was recorded that Ieyasu was greatly impressed by the bearing and demeanour of the young man.

In the light of subsequent developments it is tempting to read great significance into the conversation at Nijo Castle, which was to be the last time that the two rivals ever came face to face. Tokugawa Ieyasu was then 69 years old. His own heir Hidetada was fairly competent in his position as Shogun, but Ieyasu's continued and enormous influence on the development of Tokugawa power indicates that his confidence in Hidetada was somewhat less than total. One very reassuring factor for Ieyasu was the comforting thought that the successor of the great Hideyoshi was a mere slip of a lad who was no more the equal of his father than was Hidetada of his. Throughout Hideyori's childhood his guardian Katagiri Katsumoto had carefully propagated this myth of his effeminate weakness as a way of dissuading any disgruntled *daimyo* – and Sekigahara had provided many who fell into that category – from entertaining rebellious thoughts. If Ieyasu had ever believed in the myth himself, then the two hours he spent at Nijo Castle in 1611 completely dispelled it. Here was a unique and talented young man who, alone in Japan, had the lineage and the personality to challenge the Tokugawa. From that moment on, Hideyori's fate was sealed.

The image of Toyotomi Hideyori as effeminate and useless was carefully propagated by the Tokugawa in the years prior to Osaka. This hanging scroll continues the theme.

The great and intimidating southern wall of Osaka Castle, surrounded by the southern wet moat. This sight is little changed from 1615.

This is not to say that Ieyasu had previously ignored the potential threat from Hideyori. He had, in fact, been engaged on a long and largely successful campaign to force Hideyori to spend some of the lavish fortune that his father had amassed, much of which was sitting in Osaka Castle in the form of gold bullion. The major item of expenditure to which Hideyori was directed was the rebuilding of the Great Buddha of Kyoto. It had been Toyotomi Hideyoshi's pet project. As early as 1588, when the reunification of Japan was well in sight, Hideyoshi had conceived the idea of creating a superlative religious image for the spiritual welfare of the nation. That Japan's spiritual well-being was not the sole consideration soon became apparent when Hideyoshi set in motion his notorious 'Sword Hunt'. This was a process by which offensive weapons of all kinds were forcibly removed from minor *daimyo*, temple officials, farmers, sea captains and anyone else of whom Hideyoshi did not approve. The official line was that the weapons thus removed were to be melted down and used to provide metal bolts for the construction of the Great Buddha, but it is likely that very few were used for this purpose. Most were stockpiled and issued to the loyal *daimyo* who took part in Hideyoshi's disastrous invasions of Korea in 1592 and 1597. The Great Buddha was nevertheless constructed, only to be totally destroyed in the great earthquake of 1596. Its replacement, again for the spiritual welfare of the Japanese people, but now also as a fitting memorial to the great Hideyoshi, was an ideal pretext for emptying the coffers of Osaka. By 1602 the second image was complete up to the level of its neck, but as the workmen were engaged in casting the head early in 1603 the scaffolding caught fire and the entire statue, along with the temple that housed it, was reduced to ashes.

Work was resumed in 1608 under the supervision of Katagiri Katsumoto, and by 1612 a colossal statue of Buddha that rivalled those of Nara and Kamakura rose above the temple roofs of Japan's ancient capital. But although its construction had made a hole in the Toyotomi gold reserves, the fact that the ports of Osaka and Sakai were owned by Hideyori provided the means for his wealth to be constantly replenished. The heir of the house of Toyotomi was clearly not going to be neutralized by economics alone.

GUNPOWDER, TREASON AND PLOTS

Over the next two years Ieyasu's attitude to Hideyori changed from one of accommodation and surveillance to one of military confrontation. There is no better measure of the process than the evidence provided in the fascinating correspondence and reports of England's East India Company, which had come into being during the year that had seen the battle of Sekigahara. On 31 December 1600, Queen Elizabeth I put her signature on the Royal Charter that gave birth to the 'Company of Merchants of London trading into the East Indies' – commonly known as the East India Company (EIC). Two years later 'John Company', to use the EIC's popular nickname, was joined by 'Jan Compagnie' when the Vereenigde Oostindische Compagnie (the Dutch East India Company) was founded in Amsterdam in March 1602.

It took almost a decade for the EIC to express an interest in trade with Japan, and the first EIC vessel to sail there was the *Clove*, which reached Japan on 11 June 1613. The ship docked at Hirado, where the Dutch were already established. They provided no opposition, and the Englishmen were warmly welcomed by the local *daimyo* Matsuura Shigenobu (1549–1614). There was a short delay while they waited for William Adams to arrive, and then the party headed east to meet Tokugawa Ieyasu at Sumpu (modern Shizuoka). This audience was followed by a visit to the Shogun Tokugawa Hidetada in Edo. With the help of Adams, who had settled in Japan and become a close confidant of the Tokugawa family, the English obtained permission to trade with Japan through a 'factory' (trading post) on the island of Hirado. Among its staff were three names that we will come across in accounts of the Osaka campaign. Richard Cocks was appointed the head of the English factory in Hirado, William Eaton was based in Osaka, while Richard Wickham spent most of his time in Edo.

The political situation that existed between Ieyasu and Hideyori is first hinted at by the EIC in terms of its effects on the price of English gunpowder. In a letter from Richard Cocks in Hirado to Richard Wickham in Edo in January 1614, we read that there is 'also gunpowder, although it be under twenty *tays* the barrel, which is a low price'. Cocks nevertheless wanted the powder to be disposed of, as it was 'a dangerous commodity to be kept'. Hideyori's personal feelings of security are indicated by the fact that there was even less demand for gunpowder in Osaka. Twenty *tays* may have been regarded as a low price in Edo or Hirado, but in Osaka gunpowder was only fetching ten *tays*, as noted in a letter that William Eaton wrote to Richard Wickham on 11 March 1614. 'So at those rates I am not minded to sell as yet...' Ten *tays* was in fact the cost price of gunpowder, as revealed in an earlier letter, which lists ten barrels of gunpowder at a cost price of £3 10s 10d each. **13**

This great bronze bell provided the final excuse for Tokugawa Ieyasu to attack Toyotomi Hideyori. The two sections of the inscription that so offended Ieyasu have been picked out in white.

Late May 1614 was to find Richard Wickham in Edo writing to Cocks in Hirado and making reference to 'ordnance & powder… to put them of unto the Emperor, being only brought for him and a commodity that no man else dare buy if the Emperor once refuse them'. Richard Wickham could not have been expected to know the distinction between the remote, god-like emperor, whom the Europeans would never meet, and the real rulers of Japan: the Tokugawa Shogun and his illustrious father whom Wickham refers to as 'the Emperor'. We know that Hidetada took advantage of this exclusive gunpowder offer because of an important letter of 13 June 1614 that William Eaton wrote from Osaka to Richard Wickham in Edo:

> The powder I had here I have sent it back to Hirado… For here it will not sell, and there I make account you may put it away, as I understand … that the Emperor hath bought all you had there for 6 tays *the pecul and likewise all that the Dutch hath at Hirado at the aforesaid price, so as there is no doubt but that you may there sell it.*

This letter is very revealing about the Japanese political climate. Toyotomi Hideyori, at peace inside the safety of Osaka Castle and perceiving no threat from Ieyasu, was not at all interested in buying gunpowder from the English merchants. Eaton therefore sent his stock back to Hirado, where it was recorded in the EIC accounts as 'returned to Hirado for want of sales… 6 barrels £85 0s 0d'. However, Eaton had also found out that the Tokugawa Shogun was in the market for gunpowder in Edo. To ship it directly from Osaka to Edo might arouse suspicion, so it went via Hirado. Hidetada was nonetheless driving a hard bargain, and only paying 6 *tays* a barrel – below cost price – but the EIC appears to be satisfied.

FOR WHOM THE BELL TOLLS...

Matters were to change rapidly over the following months. With the Great Buddha complete, the only thing that remained to be done before proceeding to the final dedication of the temple was the casting of a bell. The task was begun during May 1614. A mould was built, and into it was poured a huge amount of bronze to create an enormous bell that bore, in permanent relief on its surface, an inscription in exquisite Chinese characters that was to become the death warrant for Toyotomi Hideyori.

The inscription on the bell bore the phrase *kokka anko*, 'May the state be peaceful and prosperous'. *Ka* and *ko* were the Chinese-style readings of the characters read in the Japanese style as *ie* and *yasu*, so Tokugawa Ieyasu complained that in separating the two ideographs that made up his name, Hideyori was mocking him. Elsewhere on the bell was another sentence that read 'On the east it welcomes the bright moon, on the west bids farewell to the setting sun.' This further aggrieved Ieyasu, who claimed that this alluded to him in the east of Japan as the inferior, and Hideyori the greater luminary, with a veiled threat that Hideyori intended his destruction.

It was a petty complaint, but it provided an excuse for Tokugawa Ieyasu to request Katagiri Katsumoto to act as mediator in the essentially

non-existent dispute. High-level discussions were held and, as had been intended, served only to make matters worse. It was now September 1614, and reports soon reached Edo that Hideyori was inviting unemployed and dispossessed *ronin* (lordless samurai) into Osaka Castle to provide a strengthened garrison in the case of an attack. The number of men who had been placed into this category by Ieyasu was immense, and after 14 years of obscurity and misery they had found an opening not merely for employment, but also for revenge. But Hideyori needed more than just samurai, and on 6 November William Eaton wrote from Osaka to Richard Cocks in Hirado, saying: 'I have no great matter to write you of, but only here is great inquiry now for gunpowder, and would sell at a good price. I wish I had all you have at Hirado here.' Three days later he wrote again, saying:

> *I wrote you that here was great inquiry after gunpowder, and is still very much sought after. So if you have not sold it before this comes to your hands it would not be amiss, if you think it good, to send it away for Sakai with all expedition… Powder is worth at present 26* tays *the* pecul *but I make account it will be better sold hereafter.*

So in four months the price of English gunpowder in Osaka has risen from 6 *tays* a barrel to 26 *tays*, an increase of 433 per cent. This was the highest point it was to reach, because when Richard Cocks sent a report to the EIC headquarters in London on 5 December, he recorded finally selling ten barrels of powder for 184 *tays*. It was still a good price, and he added a brief comment as to why it may be happening, because 'it is thought wars will ensue in Japan betwixt the Emperor and Fidaia Same, son to Ticus Same, the deceased Emperor.' Cocks has his titles wrong, of course, but his identification of Tokugawa Ieyasu as the emperor and Ticus Same (Taiko-sama, i.e. Toyotomi Hideyoshi) as the deceased emperor is understandable. Fidaie Same is Toyotomi Hideyori, and as the next few weeks unfolded, Richard Cocks was to have much more to report about him.

CHRONOLOGY

1593

Birth of Toyotomi Hideyori.

1598

Death of Toyotomi Hideyoshi.

1600

Battle of Sekigahara.
Dutch and English traders arrive in Japan.

1603

Tokugawa Ieyasu becomes Shogun.

The keep of Osaka Castle subsequent to its facelift in 1997.

1605

Ieyasu retires in favour of his son Hidetada.

1614

The Winter campaign of Osaka

10 October	Ieyasu receives pledges of loyalty from 50 *daimyo*.
21 October	Ikeda Tadatsugu is ordered to send troops to Amagasaki Castle.
12 November	Tokugawa Ieyasu leaves Sumpu (Shizuoka).
14 November	Katagiri Katsumoto is attacked by *ronin* at Sakai.
22 November	Date Masamune and Uesugi Kagekatsu leave Edo.
24 November	Tokugawa Ieyasu arrives in Nijo Castle in Kyoto.
	Tokugawa Hidetada leaves Edo with the main body.
6 December	Ikeda Toshitaka secures the Nakajima district.
10 December	Tokugawa Hidetada arrives at Fushimi.
15 December	Ieyasu leaves for Osaka via Nara and Horyoji.
17 December	Hidetada sets up headquarters at Hirano.
18 December	Ieyasu sets up headquarters at Sumiyoshi.
19 December	Battle of Kizugawaguchi.
26 December	Battles of Imafuku and Shigino.
29 December	Battle of Bakuroguchi.
	Battle of Noda-Fukushima.

Osaka Castle as seen from the north-east, looking from the cocktail bar of the New Otani Hotel. In the foreground is the sports hall, while at the rear is the massive NHK Television building that houses the Osaka City Museum of History.

All outposts now secured by the Eastern army. Ieyasu and Hidetada advance their headquarters to Chausuyama and Okayama.

1615

3 January 1615	Battle of the Sanada maru.
	Battle at the Hachomeguchi gate.
4 January	Battle at the Tanimachiguchi gate.
8 January	Ieyasu orders a limited bombardment of the castle.
15 January	Full artillery bombardment begins.
16 January	Night attack from castle across the Honmachi bridge.
17 January	Shot misses Hideyori but kills two ladies.
	Peace negotiations begin.
19 January	Bombardment ends.
21 January	Winter campaign officially ends with peace agreement.
22 January	Moat filling and wall demolition begin.
25 January	Ieyasu leaves Osaka for Kyoto.
8 February	Ieyasu commissions cannon from Kunitomo.
16 February	Outer moats filled in. Hidetada leaves Osaka.
13 March	Hidetada arrives in Edo.

The Summer campaign of Osaka

1 May	Ieyasu leaves Shizuoka for Nagoya.
3 May	All *daimyo* are ordered to assemble at Fushimi.
6 May	Ieyasu arrives at Nagoya for his son's wedding.
7 May	Hidetada leaves Edo.
15 May	Ieyasu arrives at Nijo Castle in Kyoto.
18 May	Hidetada arrives at Fushimi Castle.
22 May	The Eastern army is ordered to march on Osaka.
23 May	Ono Harufusa attacks Koriyama.
24 May	Ono Harufusa attacks Kamida and Horyoji on return.
25 May	Attack on Kishiwada and Sakai.
26 May	Battle of Kashii.
2 June	Ieyasu leaves for Osaka and stays the night at Hoshida.
3 June	Battle of Domyoji.
	Battle of Yao.
	Battle of Wakae.
4 June	Battle of Tennoji.
5 June	Hideyori commits suicide.

OPPOSING COMMANDERS

TOKUGAWA COMMANDERS

Tokugawa Ieyasu despite his advanced years, and the fact that he had been retired from the position of Shogun for almost ten years, remained the commander of the Tokugawa army in all but name. Born in 1542 in the castle of Okazaki, he had experienced the pain and the danger of being a child hostage, and then fought his first battles against Oda Nobunaga, the first of the three unifiers of Japan. Throughout this early period Ieyasu displayed two strong and often conflicting characteristics. The first was a headstrong willingness to lead his samurai into the thick of battle, even when the needs of his house, and his own survival, indicated caution. The second was an astute diplomacy, a mastery of psychological warfare and a feeling for grand strategy that the former characteristic often threatened to undermine. At Mikata ga Hara in 1572, for example, he unwisely engaged Takeda Shingen in battle and came very close to being killed. When forced to flee back to the safety of Hamamatsu Castle, however, he ordered the gates to be left open to fool the Takeda into thinking that a trap had been laid. The ruse worked, and Ieyasu survived to lead his army into many more encounters, where tactical caution came very much to the fore.

By the 1590s Tokugawa Ieyasu had become the master of grand strategy and practised the principle of economy of forces, using politics, diplomacy and marriage alliances as a way of keeping warfare as a last resort. But when that last resort arrived, as it did at Sekigahara in 1600, Ieyasu's role as a general on the battlefield was always a superlative one, as was his classic strategic vision. Herein lay the essence of Ieyasu's abilities and success. He possessed the particular wisdom of knowing who should be an ally and who was an enemy, and he was gifted in the broad brush strokes of a campaign. He also knew how to learn from his mistakes. Ieyasu was patient, a virtue sadly lacking in many of his contemporaries, and unlike Hideyoshi never overreached himself. Establishing his family as the ruling clan in Japan for the next two and a half centuries was abundant proof of his greatness. The destruction of Toyotomi Hideyori at Osaka was to prove the final time in his career when Ieyasu was to demonstrate his sound grasp of the principle later to be associated with the famous Prussian strategist Clausewitz: that war was the continuation of policy by other means.

Tokugawa Hidetada (1579–1632) had ruled Japan as Shogun since 1605, but although his father allowed him the honours of command of the Tokugawa army at Osaka, it is clear from all the accounts that his role was subordinate to Ieyasu, who had little confidence in him. The Sekigahara campaign had been Hidetada's first taste of action. He had

Tokugawa Ieyasu in later life, the appearance he would have had during the Summer campaign.

first been directed to take up arms against Uesugi Kagekatsu in northern Japan, but when it became clear that Ishida Mitsunari in the west was the main threat, Hidetada was ordered to hurry towards Kyoto along the Nakasendo road. On the way he commenced a siege of Ueda Castle in defiance of his father's commands, and thus arrived too late to take part in the battle of Sekigahara, a failure that could have cost them dear. Ieyasu never forgot this lapse, and Hidetada's secondary role at Osaka was certainly a consequence of it.

OSAKA COMMANDERS

Toyotomi Hideyori was the nominal commander of the Osaka army, but, unlike Hidetada, who depended upon the dominant personality of his father, Hideyori depended upon the service of a handful of loyal generals, beside whom he appears as little more than a figurehead. Hideyori's defeat would have come about much earlier had it not been for these men who, inspired by the memory of the great Hideyoshi, provided loyal service to his heir. Had any one of them been in sole command at Osaka then the direction of the campaign might have been different. As it was, their individual efforts, although often well co-ordinated, floundered because of a lack of overall vision and leadership.

Like Hidetada, Toyotomi Hideyori was the son of a famous father who had placed so much hope in him, but simply could not match the example he had been set. His father Toyotomi Hideyoshi's quest for an heir had become an obsession similar to that of England's Henry VIII. His first son, Sutemaru, had died in 1591 at the age of three. Hideyoshi then adopted as his heir his nephew Hidetsugu (1568–95), an accomplished leader of samurai, but Hidetsugu irritated him by refusing to lead the Korean invasion. In 1593 Hideyori was born, so the obstinate Hidetsugu was no longer needed, and when rumours grew of a plot against Hideyoshi he was forced to retire to Koyasan – the traditional centre of noble exile. Not long afterwards he was murdered there on Hideyoshi's instructions. When Hideyoshi died in 1598 his widow Yodogimi took young Hideyori to Osaka Castle, where he was to remain for almost the rest of his life. As noted earlier, an image of Hideyori as weak and effeminate was deliberately propagated to neutralize any role he might have had as a focus for discontent against the Tokugawa takeover. Although Ieyasu saw through it, this is the image that has come down through history: of Hideyori as the eternal child and the innocent victim. In strictly military terms, however, this myth has a great deal of truth in it. At Osaka Hideyori comes across as an indecisive and non-charismatic leader, either turning down his generals' plans with little discussion, or simply letting them do what they wanted in an unco-ordinated manner. Even his final act at Osaka, that of leading his men out of the castle for a decisive attack, was to be hopelessly botched.

Sanada Yukimura (1570–1615) was perhaps the finest of the Osaka generals. He was the son of Sanada Masayuki (1544–1608), who had served Takeda Shingen and then opposed Tokugawa Ieyasu. When Masayuki finally submitted to Ieyasu after 1586, Yukimura's elder brother Nobuyoshi (1566–1658) was sent as a hostage to Hamamatsu. Nobuyoshi

Tokugawa Hidetada, the second Tokugawa Shogun, shown in command during the Summer campaign. In reality his position was much inferior to his illustrious father's.

Sanada Yukimura, the finest general on the Osaka side and its virtual commander, shown here on a statue in Ueda, the site of one of his previous triumphs in 1600.

Goto Mototsugu, one of the greatest leaders on the Osaka side, seen here during a previous campaign on behalf of Hideyori's illustrious father Toyotomi Hideyoshi.

married the daughter of Honda Tadakatsu and went on to serve Ieyasu. This move meant that the family was split in two. Yukimura, who stayed loyal to the memory of Hideyoshi, defended Ueda Castle in 1600 against Tokugawa Hidetada. Although this was a victory, the overall defeat at Sekigahara meant that, in the great shake-up of *daimyo* domains that followed, the Sanada fief was awarded to Nobuyoshi, and Yukimura was compelled to shave his head and become a monk on Koyasan. He was there when Hideyori's call to arms was issued. Yukimura effected an escape, and joined in a final attempt to challenge the Tokugawa, while his brother Nobuyoshi fought in the siege lines against him. At Osaka Sanada Yukimura, ably assisted by his son Sanada Daisuke, became Hideyori's most reliable and gifted commander.

Goto Mototsugu (1560–1615) was another veteran campaigner who provided valuable experience for Hideyori. He had served in the Korean campaigns under Kuroda Nagamasa, where he distinguished himself at the taking of Py'ongyang in 1592, and at the battle of Chiksan in 1597, but he abandoned his master when Nagamasa inclined towards Tokugawa Ieyasu.

Kimura Shigenari (1593–1615) was one of the youngest commanders on the Osaka side. He was the son of Kimura Shigekore, who had been rewarded by Hideyoshi for his services in the Korean campaign, but had then been implicated in the alleged plot against Hideyoshi by Toyotomi Hidetsugu. As a result he was dispossessed and committed *seppuku* (suicide). In spite of this family tragedy, however, his son Shigenari stayed loyal to the name of Hideyoshi, and served Hideyori faithfully at Osaka.

OTHER COMMANDERS

To the above trio on the Osaka side we may add the names of Mori Katsunaga, once exiled by Ieyasu, and the pair of Ono Harunaga and his son Ono Harufusa. Harunaga had served Hideyoshi and had become an object of suspicion to Ieyasu, who had him exiled in the year prior to Sekigahara. Chosokabe Morichika (1575–1615) was the son of the great Motochika who had conquered all of Shikoku island, only to lose it to Hideyoshi's modern army in 1585. Finally, Akashi Morishige, who was to play a crucial role during the final operations of the Summer campaign, had been a retainer of Ukita Hideie of Bizen province, and had fought against Ieyasu at Sekigahara. Morishige was among the first to respond to Hideyori's call to arms, and became one of the few senior figures on the Osaka side to survive the campaign.

OPPOSING ARMIES

The two armies that clashed at Osaka represent the high water mark of samurai warfare in terms of the development of military technology and organization. Their numbers, and the names of their commanders, appear in the orders of battle sections. Here we will note that the basic armament of both sides was practically identical, as had been the case throughout the century of Japan's civil wars. The one exception was a considerable disparity in artillery, a matter that will be discussed later.

The Tokugawa side, often referred to as the Eastern army, was the military force of the Tokugawa Shogunate. Only a part of the whole army, however, consisted of men who were direct retainers of the Tokugawa family. The rest were the followers of the individual *daimyo*, all of whom owed their territories, and also their heads, to the decisions made about their future by Tokugawa Ieyasu after the battle of Sekigahara. In general, those who did well out of that decision were to be found besieging Osaka Castle. Those who had done badly were inside it.

On the Tokugawa side, the units that appeared within the siege lines around Osaka would have been identifiable by the flags of their commanders, who were the actual *daimyo* in the majority of cases. The numbers of men present represented a straightforward feudal obligation to supply troops for the service of the Shogun. This was a system that had long antecedents. Broadly speaking, the number of troops that a *daimyo* was required to supply depended upon the assessed wealth of his rice fields, which was measured in *koku*. One *koku* was the theoretical amount of rice needed to feed one man for one year. The troops were known as

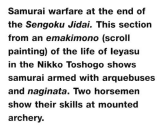

Samurai warfare at the end of the *Sengoku Jidai*. This section from an *emakimono* (scroll painting) of the life of Ieyasu in the Nikko Toshogo shows samurai armed with arquebuses and *naginata*. Two horsemen show their skills at mounted archery.

A samurai wearing a white *horo* gallops into action during the battle of Tennoji. From a painted screen depicting the siege of Osaka in the Hosei Niko Memorial Museum, Nagoya.

samurai – 'those who serve' – a reflection of the hierarchical system of obligation that had the Shogun at its apex.

Since the time of Hideyoshi, the *ashigaru* (footsoldiers) had been integrated into the standing armies of *daimyo* as the lowest ranks of samurai. They would have been armed with long spears, arquebuses or bows, while some provided attendance on the *daimyo* or on senior samurai, as grooms, weapon bearers, bodyguards, standard bearers and the like. Flag carrying was a very important task. Long banners called *nobori* were used for the identification of units, while the *daimyo*'s *uma jirushi* (literally 'horse insignia') – his battle standard – would attract some of the fiercest fighting. Only the bravest men acted as standard bearers or provided the *daimyo*'s closest attendants, and it would only be in cases of dire emergency that trained *ashigaru* would be used for menial tasks like general baggage carrying.

The *ashigaru* wore simple suits of iron armour, usually consisting of a body armour (the *do*) from which hung a skirt of protective plates. The *do* bore the *mon* (badge) of the *daimyo*, a device that also appeared on the *jingasa* (a simple lampshade-shaped helmet) and on the flags of the unit. The *ashigaru* were trained to fight in formation. The spearmen provided a defence for the missile troops, and could also act in an offensive capacity with their long spears.

The samurai were the knights of old Japan. Traditionally, they had been the only warriors to own and ride horses. Centuries earlier their primary role had been to act as mounted archers, although this skill was rarely displayed on the battlefield by 1614. Instead their usual weapon was now the spear, with which they could mount cavalry charges. The samurai's *yumi* (bow) was of made from deciduous wood faced with bamboo. Rattan binding reinforced the poor adhesive qualities of the glue used to fasten the sections together and the whole bow was lacquered to weatherproof it. The arrows were of bamboo. The archer held the bow above his head to clear the horse and then moved his hands apart as the bow was brought down to end with the left arm straight and the right hand near the right

Ii Naotaka leads the 'red devils' in a charge against Kimura Shigenari at the battle of Wakae.

ear. To release the string the fingers supporting the thumb were relaxed, at which the bow, having discharged the arrow, rotated in the hand so that it ended with the string touching the outside of the bow arm.

The *yari* (spear) carried by the mounted samurai bore little resemblance to a European knight's lance, because it was lighter and shorter and was not carried in a couched position. Its blade was very sharp on both edges, with its tang sunk into a stout oak shaft. This structure made the *yari* into a weapon unsuitable for slashing but ideal for stabbing – the best technique to use from a saddle. A useful variation was a cross-bladed spear that enabled a samurai to pull an opponent from his horse. If a samurai wished to deliver slashing strokes from horseback then a better choice than a *yari* was the *naginata*, a polearm with a long curved blade, or the spectacular *nodachi*, an extra-long sword with a very strong and very long handle. *Yari* would also be the samurai's primary weapon of choice when he had to fight dismounted, and a whole field of martial arts techniques existed for teaching its correct use.

In a siege situation like Osaka, horses were much less needed than in open battle, and in fact when the battle of Tennoji began Ieyasu ordered his men to leave their horses to the rear. Tennoji was therefore primarily a battle fought on foot, and this is reflected in the detail on the first painted screen of the Summer campaign in Osaka Castle Museum, where there are 5,071 people depicted, but only 348 horses.

The samurai's other main weapon was of course the famous *katana* – the classic samurai sword. Forged to perfection, and with a razor-sharp edge within a resilient body, this two-handed sword was the finest edged weapon in the history of warfare. Every samurai possessed at least one pair of swords, the standard fighting sword (the *katana*) and the shorter *wakizashi*. Contrary to popular belief, both seem to have been carried into battle along with a *tanto* (dagger). The samurai never used shields. Instead the *katana* was both sword and shield, its resilience enabling the samurai to deflect a blow aimed at him by knocking the attacking sword to one side with the flat of the blade and then following up with a stroke of his own.

In the press of battle the swinging of a sword was greatly restricted, and Japanese armour gave good protection, so it was rare for a man to be killed with one sweep of a sword blade unless the blow was so powerful that it split an opponent's helmet in two. Sword fighting from a horse was not easy, because the normally two-handed *katana* then had to be used in one hand, but this disadvantage was somewhat overcome by the samurai's position above a footsoldier and the momentum of his horse. The curvature of the sword's blade, which allowed the very hard and very sharp cutting edge to slice into an opponent along a small area, would open up to cut through to the bone as the momentum of the swing continued. Historical records show that some samurai survived multiple cuts from sword blades. One victim was still alive after 13 strokes found their mark, and on a separate occasion a horse endured seven slashes.

The samurai's suit of armour was stronger and more elaborate than that of the humbler *ashigaru*. By 1615 the traditional style of manufacture, whereby the armour plates were made from individual iron scales laced together, had been modified to allow solid-plate body armours that gave better protection against gunfire. Lamellar sections, however, continued to be found in the *haidate* (thigh guards) and *sode* (shoulder guards). Armoured sleeves for the arm and shinguards protected those areas of the body. Above the neck could be found the most striking part of a samurai's armour – an iron mask that protected the face (it also provided a secure point for tying the helmet cords). The mask was often decorated with moustaches made of horsehair, and the mouthpiece might well sport a sinister grin around white teeth.

The helmet was a very solid affair, but senior samurai, and many *daimyo*, would use the design of the helmet crown to give a personal touch to what was otherwise a very practical outfit. Wood and papier mâché were used to build up the surface of an iron helmet into fantastic shapes. Buffalo horns, seashells, catfish tails and antlers were among the many weird and wonderful devices that graced the appearance of a proud samurai.

The other way in which an individual samurai would be recognized in the heat of battle was by wearing on his back a small identifying device called a *sashimono*. This was often a flag in a wooden holder. An *ashigaru*'s *sashimono* would be simply a means of unit recognition by means of the *daimyo*'s *mon* on a coloured background. This system would be the case for most rank and file samurai too, but senior samurai would be allowed to have their own *mon*, or sometimes their surname displayed on the flag. Golden fans and plumes of feathers could replace the small flag, while the most spectacular form of *sashimono* was the curious *horo*. This was a cloak stretched over a bamboo framework and had supposedly originated as an arrow catcher, but by the time of the Age of Warring States it had become a decorative appendage for a *daimyo*'s elite samurai who acted as his bodyguards or messengers. The *horo* filled with air as the samurai rode across the battlefield, and the bright colours made him easily recognizable to friend and foe. It was customary that when a *horo*-wearing samurai was decapitated his head was wrapped in the *horo* for presentation as a mark of respect.

All descriptions of the actions at Osaka confirm that the troops supplied by the *daimyo* were not mixed up together in one huge army, but fought instead in *daimyo*-led divisions, linked by common experience of fighting together, and with many family and marriage ties at the top end of the command structure to provide a cohesive social glue. Any weapon specialization fell within that identifiable unit.

This arrangement was similar on both sides, but the structure of Toyotomi Hideyori's Osaka army was made more complicated by the presence of thousands of *ronin*. At the core of Hideyori's force was an army that consisted of his personal retainers. Some of these provided his bodyguard, while others occupied a station inside the defensive walls. Certain *daimyo* present at Osaka had armies of their own, and had simply defied Ieyasu's command to serve the Shogun. But many of the names that appear on the map of the siege were not commanding men to whom they had a long-lasting obligation. Instead their followers were the *ronin* who had flocked into the castle, and were placed under reliable command. In such a way did men who had once been *daimyo* with armies of their own suddenly became something very similar again as the Tokugawa drew near. Most of the *ronin* under their command would probably have been indistinguishable from 'regular' samurai, but some would have been impoverished characters, a fate reflected in their appearance as much as it was in their uninhibited fighting.

THE WINTER CAMPAIGN

As the Winter and Summer campaigns of Osaka were totally different in nature, they will be discussed in two separate sections, one for each of the operations.

OPPOSING PLANS

Tokugawa Ieyasu's plans

Once he had goaded Hideyori into taking defensive measures in Osaka, Tokugawa Ieyasu moved from a position of exerting political pressure to one of overt military action. His plans for what was to become the Winter campaign were very straightforward. Being in possession of Fushimi and Nijo castles in Kyoto, he needed to move the bulk of his army from Edo under Hidetada, and from Sumpu under his own command, to these two places ready for the final advance against Osaka Castle. Meanwhile, other *daimyo* would secure positions around Osaka and make themselves ready to join the siege lines when the order came.

The castle's position, with sea to the west, mountains to the east and rivers to the north, meant that the Tokugawa army could approach Osaka from Kyoto by two routes: along the line of the Yodogawa via Ibaraki Castle, or from the direction of Nara, sheltered by the Ikoma mountain

The view from the keep of Osaka Castle looking north-east across the north outer moat to the confluence of two of the rivers in their modern channels that still form the castle's 'outer moat'. We see the Gokurabashi that provides the only access to the north from the Hon maru, and the Aoya gate, site of the former Aoyaguchi. Behind this gate is the modern sports hall.

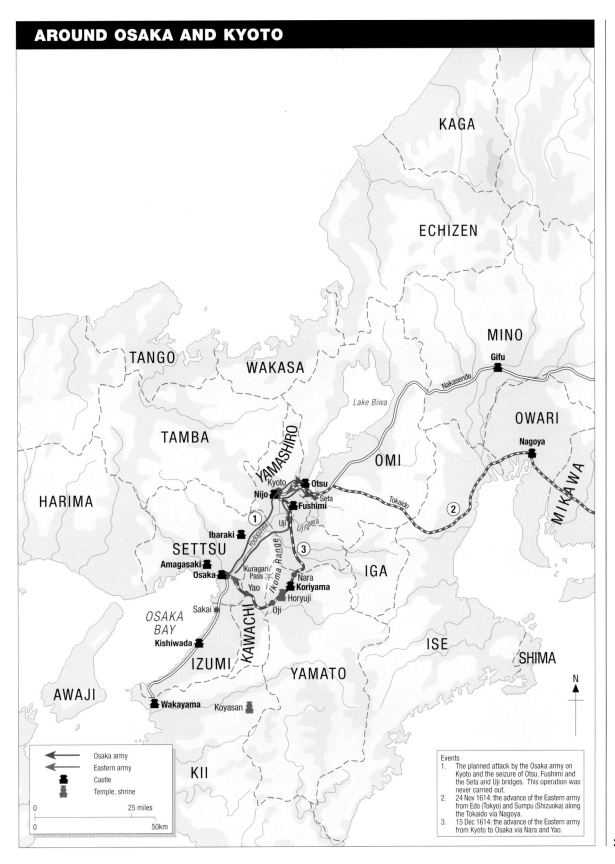

KAGA

ECHIZEN

MINO

Gifu

OWARI

Nagoya

TANGO

WAKASA

Nakasendo

Lake Biwa

TAMBA

YAMASHIRO

OMI

HARIMA

Kyoto   Otsu
Nijo   Seta
Fushimi
Tokaido

MIKAWA

SETTSU

Ibaraki

Uji   Ujigawa

IGA

Amagasaki
Osaka
Yao

Kuragari Pass
Ikoma Range

Nara
Koriyama
Horyuji

ISE

SHIMA

OSAKA BAY

Sakai

Oji

KAWACHI

YAMATO

Kishiwada

IZUMI

N

AWAJI

Wakayama   Koyasan

KII

Events

1. The planned attack by the Osaka army on Kyoto and the seizure of Otsu, Fushimi and the Seta and Uji bridges. This operation was never carried out.
2. 24 Nov 1614: the advance of the Eastern army from Edo (Tokyo) and Sumpu (Shizuoka) along the Tokaido via Nagoya.
3. 15 Dec 1614: the advance of the Eastern army from Kyoto to Osaka via Nara and Yao.

Osaka army
Eastern army
Castle
Temple, shrine

0   25 miles
0   50km

range. If advancing by the latter route, Ieyasu would turn west over the mountains at some point towards Osaka, or make a wider sweep through Nara, Horyoji and Oji, cutting through the mountains at Domyoji, where the Yamatogawa flowed. The open expanse of ground to the south of the castle, where the defences were lightest (a matter discussed in detail below) would provide the best base from which to conduct a siege.

Toyotomi Hideyori's plans

Nothing shows the lack of unified leadership among the Osaka garrison better than the failure to agree a strategy against the Tokugawa threat. Hideyori essentially had two choices. One was to sit inside Osaka Castle and allow Ieyasu to come to him. The other was to take the fight to the Tokugawa in some way, or at the very least to impede their progress westwards.

Sanada Yukimura and Goto Mototsugu proposed means towards an offensive campaign, and took note of the points discussed above of how the Tokugawa army would approach Osaka. The journey towards Kyoto from the east also allowed certain possibilities for the Tokugawa to be intercepted on the way. The coast road (the Tokaido) and the road through the central mountains (the Nakasendo) joined together shortly before Lake Biwa. From this point all traffic flowed across the Seta bridge, which crossed the Ujigawa as it left the lake. If Kyoto could be secured as well as Seta then the Tokugawa advance would be neutralized. Ishida Mitsunari had attempted a similar strategy in 1600. He had captured the castles of Otsu and Fushimi, and with his rear secure, fought Ieyasu at Sekigahara on the Nakasendo.

With this in mind, Sanada Yukimura and Goto Mototsugu proposed a very bold strategy. While retaining Osaka Castle as a place of safety to which they could retreat if necessary, two armies should advance to secure the approach roads. The first, smaller, force should head east to win control of the Nara passes. The second should secure Ibaraki, and then go on to take Fushimi and then Kyoto itself. There they would secure Nijo Castle and then the imperial palace. With the august emperor in their hands, Tokugawa Ieyasu could be declared a rebel against the throne. This was a strategy that had been adopted on several occasions during the 12th-century wars between the Taira and the Minamoto. Imperial approval would encourage any wavering *daimyo* to cast their lots with the cause of the dispossessed Toyotomi Hideyori. Taking the bridge at Seta, across which passed the combined roads from the east, would complete the control of the area of the capital. The Tokugawa 'rebels' would go no further.

This elaborate plan was never put into action. Instead, Hideyori decided to sit tight inside Osaka Castle and allow the Tokugawa a free passage almost to the edge of his defensive line.

ORDERS OF BATTLE

An army list for the Winter campaign is included in *Osaka no jin* (Volume 40 in the Rekishi Gunzo Series). It shows the Osaka garrison before the loss of Imafuku and Noda-Fukushima to be distributed around the defences as follows:

Hon maru (inner bailey)	3,080
Ni no maru (second bailey) – east	5,000
Ni no maru (second bailey) – south	22,300
Ni no maru (second bailey) – west	12,800
Ni no maru (second bailey) – north	11,000
Nekomagawa	5,000
Southern new wall	15,000
Ikutama Canal	8,600
Tenmagawa bank	7,900
Sanada maru	5,000
Imafuku	2,600
Kizugawa	1,500
Noda-Fukushima	13,300
Total:	113,080

The author, however, adds a note that the numbers within the Ni no maru may include 23,000 reserves, thus giving a more likely total of 90,080. As the numbers of *ronin* cannot be known for certain, a rough estimate of about 100,000 men inside Osaka Castle is probably a workable figure.

Overall figures for the Tokugawa side are as follows, according to the points of the compass and position around the castle:

East – Hiranogawa	14,500
South – Tennoji	46,100
South-west – Kizugawa	10,000
West – Ikutama Canal	45,700
North-west – Noda-Fukushima	2,000
North – Yodogawa	17,100
North-east – Kyoto road	2,000
Okayama (Tokugawa Hidetada)	20,000
Chausuyama (Tokugawa Ieyasu)	30,000
Others	7,000
Total:	194,400

The keep of Osaka Castle, viewed through the Sakura gate.

This figure does not include Shimazu Iehisa's 30,000 samurai, who arrived too late to take part in the Winter campaign. Overall, the Tokugawa army outnumbered the Osaka garrison by two to one.

A finer breakdown is possible for certain contingents. In the list of names that follow, the Eastern, or Tokugawa army commanders are all *daimyo* commanding samurai who have an obligation to them under the feudal system, just as the *daimyo* have an obligation in turn to the Shogun. Apart from the 'household troops' of the Tokugawa, the largest contingent (12,000) was supplied by Maeda Toshitsune, the richest *daimyo* in Japan under the Tokugawa. His contribution worked out at 8.5 men per 1,000 *koku*. No named contribution on the Tokugawa side was less than 60 men. In the case of the Osaka army, however, many of the commanders named are there in a personal capacity and have been put in charge of a number of *ronin*: men, like them, without a master to follow.[1]

Eastern army

For the convenience of the reader, each of the following contingents has been given the number that appears on the key of the map on p.38.

1. Tokugawa Ieyasu	30,000
2. Tokugawa Hidetada	20,000
3. Maeda Toshitsune	12,000
4. Matsukura Shigemasa	200
5. Sakakibara Yasukatsu	300
6. Kuwayama Kazunao	600
7. Furuta Shigeharu	1,000
8. Wakizaka Yasumoto	500
9. Terazawa Hirotaka	500
10. Ii Naotaka	4,000
11. Matsudaira Tadanao	10,000
12. Todo Takatora	4,000
13. Date Masamune	10,000
14. Date Hidemune	(included with Masamune)
15. Mori Hidenari	10,000
16. Tokunaga Masashige	(included under Mori Hidenari)
17. Fukushima Masakatsu	(included under Mori Hidenari)
18. Asano Nagaakira	7,000
19. Togawa Michiyasu	7,000
20. Yamauchi Tadayoshi	5,000
21. Matsudaira Tadaaki	5,000
22. Hachisuka Yoshishige	5,000
23. Ikeda Tadakatsu	5,000
24. Inaba Norimichi	1,200
25. Nabeshima Katsushige	7000
26. Ishikawa Tadafusa	300
27. Ikeda Tadatsugu	8,800
28. Mori Tadamasa	800
29. Arima Naozumi	600
30. Tachibana Muneshige	300
31. Wakebe Mitsunobu	(included under Tachibana Muneshige)
32. Honda Tadamasa	3,000
33. Arima Toyouji	800
34. Ikeda Toshitaka	8,000
35. Nakagawa Hisashige	600
36. Kato Akinari	600
37. Matsudaira Yasushige	1,500
38. Okabe Nagamori	(included under Matsudaira Yasushige)

[1] There is no space here to include full details of the heraldry of the *daimyo*, where this is known. Some lesser-known flags have been deliberately included in the colour plates, and many more Osaka combatants appear in *Samurai Heraldry* (Osprey Elite 82), particularly Plate J, where the unlabelled Number 12 is the flag of Matsushita Shigetsuna. More flags used at Osaka may be found in the reproductions of the Winter campaign screen in *Samurai Warfare* (Arms and Armour Press, 1996) and *The Samurai Sourcebook* (Cassell, 1998).

39. Nose Katsukiyo	see subtotal below
40. Seki Kazumasa	see subtotal below
41. Takenaka Shigekado	see subtotal below
42. Bessho Yoshiharu	see subtotal below
43. Ichihashi Nagakatsu	commanders 39–43: total 1,700
44. Hasegawa Moritomo	see subtotal below
45. Honda Yasunori	see subtotal below
46. Miyagi Toyomori	see subtotal below
47. Makita Yasusada	see subtotal below
48. Katagiri Katsumoto	see subtotal below
49. Katagiri Sadamasa	see subtotal below
50. Ishikawa Sadamasa	see subtotal below
51. Kinoshita Nobutoshi	see subtotal below
52. Hanabusa Masanari	see subtotal below
53. Hanabusa Masamori	commanders 44–53: total 2,000
54. Asano Nagashige	200
55. Sanada Nobuyoshi	700
56. Sanada Nobumasa	(included under Nobuyoshi)
57. Satake Yoshinobu	1,500
58. Honda Tadatomo	300
59. Uesugi Kagekatsu	5,000
60. Niwa Nagashige	200
61. Horio Tadaharu	800
62. Toda Ujinobu	1,000
63. Makino Tadanari	500
64. Akita Sanesue	700
65. Honda Yasutoshi	300
66. Uemura Yasukatsu	300
67. Koide Yoshichika	300
68. Matsushita Shigetsuna	200
69. Sengoku Tadamasa	300
70. Sakai Ietsugu	1,200
71. Mizutani Katsutaka	500
72. Koide Yoshifusa	500
73. Nambu Toshinao	3,000
74. Kuki Moritaka	800
75. Mukai Tadakatsu	(included under Kuki Moritaka)
76. Hanabusa Motoyuki	(included under Kuki Moritaka)

Osaka army

For the convenience of the reader, each of the following contingents has been given the number that appears on the key of the map on p.38.

1. Toyotomi Hideyori	3,080
2. Inagi Norikazu	(included under Toyotomi Hideyori)
3. Asai Nagafusa	3,000
4. Miura Yoshitsugu	(included under Asai Nagafusa)
5. Oda Nagayori	1,300
6. Yuasa Masahisa	2,000
7. Chosokabe Morichika	5,000
8. Goto Mototsugu	3,000
9. Aoki Nobushige	1,000
10. Watanabe Tadasu	500
11. Makishima Shigetoshi	1,500
12. Najima Tadamune	1,300
13. Mori Katsunaga	5,000
14. Hayami Morihisa	4,000
15. Hotta Masataka	3,000
16. Ikoma Masazumi	800
17. Ono Harunaga	1,300 (plus 5,000 rapid reserve corps)
18. Ono Harufusa	5,000

19. Sanada Yukimura	5,000
20. Nambu Nobutsura	1,500
21. Nogamura Yoshiyasu	1,200
22. Sanada Daisuke	(included under Sanada Yukimura)
23. Hideyori's direct retainers	3,000
24. Toda Tameshige	(included under Akashi Morishige)
25. Sengoku Munenori	(included under Akashi Morishige)
26. Akashi Morishige	2,000
27. Ishikawa Sadanori	(included under Yamakawa Katanobu)
28. Yamakawa Katanobu	4,000
29. Kimura Shigenari	8,000
30. Kori Yoshitsura	(included under Chosokabe Morichika)
31. Nakajima Ujitane	2,000
32. Naito Tadatoyo	2,000
33. Inoue Tokitoshi	3,300
34. Kitagawa Nobukatsu	(included under Inoue Tokitoshi)
35. Sano Yorizutsu	1,000
36. Kurokawa Sadatane	300
37. Akaza Naonori	300
38. Takamatsu Naisho	1,300
39. Kawasaki Izumi	(included under Takamatsu Naisho)
40. Ito Nagatsugu	3,000
41. Ban Naotsugu	150
42. Akashi Teruzumi	2,000
43. Susukida Kanesuke	700 at Bakuroguchi
44. Yano Masanori	300 at Imafuku
45. Iida Iesada	300 at Imafuku

THE DEFENCES OF OSAKA

As far as Tokugawa Ieyasu was concerned, the Winter campaign of Osaka began when Toyotomi Hideyori was seen to be extending the defences of his castle and packing it with *ronin*, two operations that served to enhance the already formidable structure that was Osaka Castle.

Osaka Castle

Osaka Castle owed its foundation to Rennyo Shonin (1415–99), the great patriarch and reformer of the Jodo Shinsho (True Pure Land) sect of Buddhism, from whom were drawn the militant Ikko-ikki (Single-minded League) armies. When he retired from their leadership in 1489, Rennyo yearned for peace and tranquillity, which he was to find a few years later in a rustic hermitage at a place known as 'the great slope' i.e. *o saka*. He did not have long to enjoy peace and quiet, because his adoring followers sought him out, and before long the simple hermitage had been replaced by a temple called Ishiyama Honganji, which was soon surrounded by a town. By the 1530s the determination of successive *daimyo* to crush the Ikko-ikki had led to the place being fortified. After a long war against Oda Nobunaga, Ishiyama Honganji surrendered in 1580, and a few years later it became the site of Hideyoshi's Osaka Castle.

The 'great slope' that gave Osaka its name begins its incline from south to north in the area of the modern Tennoji Station, and terminates in a plateau beside the Tenma River where the castle is located. Although it is now within a huge modern city, there are a few places where the slope may still be discerned. Place names mentioned in accounts of the Osaka campaign may also be found within the bustling metropolis.

This view of the south outer moat of Osaka Castle shows the fine detail of the massive stone blocks that make up a classic example of the sloping stone fortifications of a Japanese castle.

A splendid view of Osaka Castle from the south-west, spoiled only by a slight reflection in the windows of the Osaka City Museum of History. The ramp across to the castle is the Oteguchi, leading to a 90-degree turn through the Ote gate. Access to the Hon maru is provided by the Sakura gate at the far right of the picture.

The Tenma River was but one branch of a complex delta that provided a set of natural moats for Osaka Castle on its northern side. The main feed was the Yodogawa, formed from the Ujigawa (which drained Lake Biwa) and other tributaries. Today the Yodogawa has been directed into a massive channel somewhat to the north of the Tenmagawa. In 1614 this channel was known as the Nakatsugawa, while the Yodogawa flowed in a curve round towards the castle. This complex river system was, and still is, Osaka Castle's first natural moat to the north. Beyond was a maze of islands and creeks, crossed by bridges. Where the Yodogawa joined the Yamatogawa was a small island called Bizenjima, and just to the south of it the main road to Kyoto crossed the river by a bridge known as Kyobashi. To the east flowed a small river called the Nekomagawa, which became Osaka's outer moat in that direction. Beyond the Nekomagawa was the Hiranogawa, joined in 1614 by the Yamatogawa, a further main river to the east that does not exist today. (The Yamatogawa, which flows down from the hills of Nara, was redirected in 1673 to flow directly westwards to join the sea at Sakai.) The main area of the *jokamachi* (castle

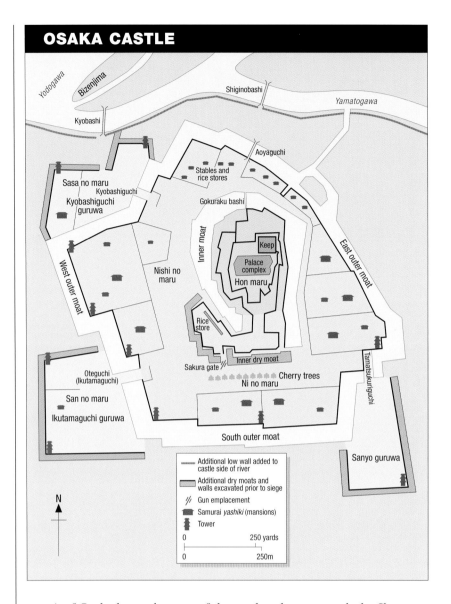

town) of Osaka lay to the west of the castle, where a canal, the Ikutama, had been cut between the Tenmagawa and the sea. It ran from north to south, then turned sharply west to join the Kizugawa. Within its boundaries lived thousands of people, who continued with their lives as far as possible while the siege progressed.

With rivers or canals at three points of the compass, only the southern side lay open to attack. It was accordingly decided to cut a ditch between the Nekomagawa and the Ikutama Canal. It does not seem to have been a wet moat, because there was not enough time for the extra engineering that this would have required. Instead it was a wide, dry ditch, reinforced with palisades. A wall of earth and stone was constructed on its inner side, with gateways protected by angled walls at the points where major roads left the castle. At the eastern end of the new ditch, a barbican was constructed. Named the Sanada maru after the illustrious Sanada Yukimura, it consisted of a half-moon shaped earthwork with wooden walls.

The view from the keep of Osaka Castle looking south.

A rare detail showing the roof of the *yashiki* (palace complex) of Osaka Castle. It lies within the wall of the Hon maru, which is shown as a mixture of black-painted wood and white plaster. From the painted screen depicting the Summer campaign of Osaka in Osaka Castle Museum.

The inner defences of Osaka

The heart of Osaka's defences, however, was the complex of keep, palace and inner walls with moats that Toyotomi Hideyoshi had built over the ashes of Ishiyama Honganji, and in spite of the passage of centuries the overall layout is largely preserved to this day. Its appearance in 1614 is shown in the map on p.34. There was first of all a wet outer moat with massive stone walls on its inner sides. It was split up by four fortified ramps that allowed access to the inner castle. They were known as the Kyobashiguchi, the Aoyaguchi, the Tamatsukuriguchi and the Oteguchi (or Ikutamaguchi). Each had a massive gatehouse on the inner side. Prior to the siege, all but the Aoyaguchi (which faced the rivers at the north) had extra defences added to them in the form of simple open areas protected all round by walls and dry moats, with towers at all corners. The new defences around the Kyobashiguchi, which covered the approach to the castle across the Kyobashi bridge along the main road towards Kyoto, were called the Sasa no guruwa. As the south side of the castle was the most vulnerable direction for attack, the two approach ramps lay at the two corners of the southern wet moat. An attacker approaching from the south would therefore see nothing but a deep, wide water-filled moat covered by huge stone walls, a stunning example of fortification little changed to this day. The new defences around them were known respectively as the Sanyo guruwa and the Ikutamaguchi guruwa.

Within the outer wet moat lay the Ni no maru, or 'second bailey' of the castle. Most of its area, particularly the western side or Nishi no maru (western bailey), was a flat expanse of ground, with various buildings, each defended by low walls around the edges. Their functions included residences for samurai, rice stores and stables. Between the Ni no maru and the castle's innermost area – the Hon maru (main or inner bailey) – was another wet moat. It was horseshoe shaped with its open side to the south. Here the Osaka garrison excavated a further dry moat, and a gap across it provided one of only two means of access to the Hon maru. Its formidable gate was known as the Sakura mon from the line of cherry trees that grew in front of it. A bridge, known as the Gokuraku bashi (paradise bridge) at the most northerly point of the horseshoe, provided the only other entrance point to the Hon maru.

On passing through the Sakura gate a visitor would have found two more circuits of stone walls, each forming an outer skin to successive layers of the castle mound, excavated in traditional Japanese fashion from the 'great slope' of Osaka. The innermost wall enclosed a magnificent palace complex, the *yashiki*, nothing of which has survived. The *yashiki* would have been a one-storey building of reception rooms, living quarters and support functions for Hideyori and his closest circle. In a design common to all *daimyo*'s castles, the rooms would have been floored with *tatami* (straw mats) and linked by polished wooden corridors. Each room could be subdivided by lavishly decorated sliding wooden panels, while the walls immediately adjacent to the outside corridors would have been *shoji*, sliding translucent panels, with weatherproof wooden shutters that could be lowered at night. The Jesuit missionary Luis Frois was very impressed by Osaka's *yashiki*, which he described as 'sumptuous and lovely', set off by the exquisite gardens around it and a 'delightful' tea house.

At the north-eastern corner of the palace complex lay Osaka's keep, which also impressed Luis Frois, who was privileged to have a guided tour led by Toyotomi Hideyoshi himself in 1586. It was the highest point of the whole castle and was visible from a vast distance away. When Tokugawa Ieyasu rebuilt Osaka Castle after the siege a new keep of a very different size and shape was raised in another place within the Hon maru. This survived until the fighting of the Meiji Restoration in 1868, and when the keep was rebuilt in 1931 it was decided to recreate Hideyoshi's original version. It was refurbished in 1997, and the major source for its appearance was one

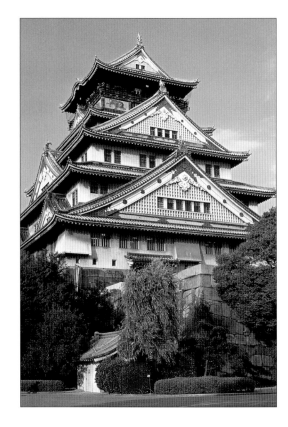

The keep of Osaka Castle, rebuilt according to the dimensions of the original keep that saw the siege of Osaka.

The flag of Toyotomi Hideyori, with the *mon* (badge) of the paulownia plant, still flies defiantly from the entrance to the keep of Osaka Castle. A small window and stone-dropping 'machicolations' may also be seen.

of the two painted screens of the Summer campaign that are owned by Osaka Castle Museum. The keep may be found in the upper left-hand corner of the screen. It had six storeys above the level of the stone base and two below it. It was built of wood, each floor having a central open area, with corridors and staircases on the outer edges. The decoration of the outside, with golden cranes and tigers, proclaimed the glory of Hideyoshi in no uncertain fashion.

SECURING POSITIONS

By 17 December 1614, Richard Cocks of the EIC was sufficiently well informed of the developing situation in Osaka to write to John Saris in England, saying that Toyotomi Hideyori:

> … hath fortified himself strongly in his castle or fortress of Osaka, having eighty thousand or an hundred thousand men, runaways and banished men, malcontents, which are retired out of all parts unto him and victualled themselves for three years. The old Emperor himself is come down against him in person with an army of three hundred thousand soldiers… their forerunners have had two or three bickerings already and many slain on each part. All Osaka is burned to the ground except the castle.

The above passage provides a very good summary of the events that took place between October and early December 1614, which we will now examine in detail.

The Tokugawa advance to Osaka: October–November 1614

As tension mounted and the increased defences of Osaka grew in size, both sides began to secure support. By 10 October Tokugawa Ieyasu had received pledges of loyalty from 50 *daimyo*, and 11 days later one of them had an audience with him at Sumpu that was probably not atypical. Ikeda Toshitaka (1584–1616) was the lord of the famous castle of Himeji, and was ordered to move his samurai to reinforce the castle of Amagasaki, a fortress that lay just to the west of Osaka. This was the beginning of a strategy whereby certain *daimyo* whose fiefs lay near to Osaka secured key strongpoints in a broad curve running from Amagasaki in the west, through Ibaraki in the north and Koriyama in the east, to Kishiwada along the coast to the south. On 12 November Tokugawa Ieyasu left Sumpu at the head of his household troops.

The first shots of the Osaka campaign were probably fired during a minor skirmish on 14 November at Sakai, the port that lay to the south of Osaka. On that date Katagiri Katsumoto, sent to reinforce the Tokugawa presence at Sakai, arrived to find the place under the control of Hideyori's *ronin*, who attacked him with great vigour. This action is probably the basis for a report that appears in a letter of the East India Company where concern is expressed about the safety of the EIC traders in Osaka and Sakai, because, 'Master Baton is gone to Sakai with his goods; yet not without danger, for part of that town is burned too'.

It was a foretaste of the reception that awaited the rest of the Tokugawa army, which was soon on its way eastwards in full strength.

FUKUSHIMA

NAKAJIMA

IMAFUKU

NODA

To Kyoto

Yodogawa

To Kyoto

Yamatogawa

SHIGINO

Nakanoshima

Bizenjima

Tenmagawa

Nekomagawa

74, 75, 76
(Guardships)

Ikutama Canal

Shima Bakuro

Bakuroguchi

Ashijima

Yetazaki

Kizugawa

Sanada maru

Sasayama
(20m)

Hiranogawa

To Nara

To Nara

Osaka Bay

Shitennoji Temple

Chausuyama
(26m)

Okayama
(25.5m)

To Yao

1 mile

- ▬▬ Outer and supplementary walls
- Eastern army
- Osaka army
- ← Eastern artillery operations
- ← Osaka artillery range
- ⚡ Artillery emplacement

0 ___ 1 mile

0 ___ 1km

Eastern army			
1. Tokugawa Ieyasu	22. Hachisuka Yoshishige	43. Ichihashi Nagakatsu	64. Akita Sanesue
2. Tokugawa Hidetada	23. Ikeda Tadakatsu	44. Hasegawa Moritomo	65. Honda Yasutoshi
3. Maeda Toshitsune	24. Inaba Norimichi	45. Honda Yasunori	66. Uemura Yasukatsu
4. Matsukura Shigemasa	25. Nabeshima Katsushige	46. Miyagi Toyomori	67. Koide Yoshichika
5. Sakakibara Yasukatsu	26. Ishikawa Tadafusa	47. Makita Yasusada	68. Matsushita Shigetsuna
6. Kuwayama Kazunao	27. Ikeda Tadatsugu	48. Katagiri Katsumoto	69. Sengoku Tadamasa
7. Furuta Shigeharu	28. Mori Tadamasa	49. Katagiri Sadamasa	70. Sakai Ietsugu
8. Wakizaka Yasumoto	29. Arima Naozumi	50. Ishikawa Sadamasa	71. Mizutani Katsutaka
9. Terazawa Hirotaka	30. Tachibana Muneshige	51. Kinoshita Nobutoshi	72. Koide Yoshifusa
10. Ii Naotaka	31. Wakebe Mitsunobu	52. Hanabusa Masanari	73. Nambu Toshinao
11. Matsudaira Tadanao	32. Honda Tadamasa	53. Hanabusa Masamori	74. Kuki Moritaka
12. Todo Takatora	33. Arima Toyouji	54. Asano Nagashige	75. Mukai Tadakatsu
13. Date Masamune	34. Ikeda Toshitaka	55. Sanada Nobuyoshi	76. Hanabusa Motoyuki
14. Date Hidemune	35. Nakagawa Hisashige	56. Sanada Nobumasa	
15. Mori Hidenari	36. Kato Akinari	57. Satake Yoshinobu	**Osaka army**
16. Tokunaga Masashige	37. Matsudaira Yasushige	58. Honda Tadatomo	1. Toyotomi Hideyori
17. Fukushima Masakatsu	38. Okabe Nagamori	59. Uesugi Kagekatsu	(household and
18. Asano Nagaakira	39. Nose Katsukiyo	60. Niwa Nagashige	bodyguard)
19. Togawa Michiyasu	40. Seki Kazumasa	61. Horio Tadaharu	2. Inagi Norikazu
20. Yamauchi Tadayoshi	41. Takenaka Shigekado	62. Toda Ujinobu	3. Asai Nagafusa
21. Matsudaira Tadaaki	42. Bessho Yoshiharu	63. Makino Tadanari	4. Miura Yoshitsugu

5. Oda Nagayori	25. Sengoku Munenori
6. Yuasa Masahisa	26. Akashi Morishige
7. Chosokabe Morichika	27. Ishikawa Sadanori
8. Goto Mototsugu	28. Yamakawa Katanobu
9. Aoki Nobushige	29. Kimura Shigenari
10. Watanabe Tadasu	30. Kori Yoshitsura
11. Makishima Shigetoshi	31. Nakajima Ujitane
12. Najima Tadamune	32. Naito Tadatoyo
13. Mori Katsunaga	33. Inoue Tokitoshi
14. Hayami Morihisa	34. Kitagawa Nobukatsu
15. Hotta Masataka	35. Sano Yorizutsu
16. Ikoma Masazumi	36. Kurokawa Sadatane
17. Ono Harunaga	37. Akaza Naonori
18. Ono Harufusa	38. Takamatsu Naisho
19. Sanada Yukimura	39. Kawasaki Izumi
20. Nambu Nobutsura	40. Ito Nagatsugu
21. Nogamura Yoshiyasu	41. Ban Naotsugu
22. Sanada Daisuke	42. Akashi Teruzumi
23. Toyotomi Hideyori	
(retainers)	
24. Toda Tameshige	

Events

1. Mid Nov: The Osaka garrison excavates a dry moat and raises a wall between the Ikutama Canal and the Nekomagawa. A barbican, the Sanada maru, is added, and the inner castle defences extended.
2. 6 Dec: Ikeda Toshitaka secures the Nakajima area.
3. 17 Dec: Tokugawa Hidetada sets up temporary headquarters at Hirano.
4. 18 Dec: Tokugawa Ieyasu sets up temporary headquarters at Sumiyoshi.
5. 19 Dec: Hachisuka Yoshishige, Asano Nagaakira and Ikeda Tadakatsu capture the fort of Kizugawaguchi from Akashi Teruzumi.
6. 26 Dec: Uesugi Kagekatsu captures the fort of Shigino from Inoue Yoritsugu but is attacked by Ono Harunaga and has to be reinforced.
7. 26 Dec: Satake Yoshinobu captures three forts at Imafuku from Yano Masanori and Iida Iesada, but is attacked by Kimura Shigenari and Goto Mototsugu.
8. 29 Dec: Crossing from Ashijima, Ishikawa Tadafusa captures the fort of Bakuroguchi from Susukida Kanesuke, assisted by Hachisuka Yoshishige.
9. 29 Dec: Battle of Noda-Fukushima. Kuki Moritaka secures the estuary beside the Noda fort. The fort of Fukushima is taken by Ikeda Tadatsugu moving overland.
10. Early January: With all the outposts secure, Ieyasu and Hidetada advance their headquarters to Chausuyama and Okayama respectively.
11. 3 Jan: On being warned of an attack by Maeda Toshitsune, Sanada Yukimura pulls back from the hill of Sasayama to the Sanada maru.
12. 3 Jan: Ii Naotaka and Matsudaira Tadanao attack the Sanada maru but are driven off. They then break through the Hachomeguchi gate but are driven back by Kimura Shigenari, who then sallies out.
13. 4 Jan: Todo Takatora enters the Tanimachiguchi gate, but is driven out by Chosokabe Morichika.
14. 16 Jan: In response to the initial artillery bombardment, a surprise night attack is launched across the Honmachi bridge by Ban Naotsugu.

NOTE:
The area is remarkably flat except for the three tiny hills! However, 'Osaka' means 'big slope'. The original slope was from north to south, from Sasayama up to a 'cliff' on the Tenma River. By the time the castle had been built the excavations for the castle mounds hid the slope, but it can still be seen today as a gentle incline.

Legend:
— Outer and supplementary walls
⊏⊐ Ditches and dry moats
← Eastern (Tokugama) army
← Osaka (Toyotomi) army

0 ___ 1 mile
0 ___ 1km

Two great northern *daimyo*, Date Masamune (1566–1636) the 'one-eyed dragon' from Sendai, and Uesugi Kagekatsu (1555–1623) from Yonezawa began the procession from Edo. The latter had opposed Ieyasu at Sekigahara and paid for his folly by having his territory exchanged for another, but by the time of Osaka his submission was complete. He was followed by Satake Yoshinobu (1570–1633), who had also survived the upheaval of Sekigahara with the loss of territory and a certain dignity. Two days later, on the same day that Ieyasu arrived safely inside Nijo Castle in Kyoto, his son Tokugawa Hidetada also left Edo with the main body of the Tokugawa samurai.

By 10 December all the Tokugawa samurai had arrived unhindered and unmolested from the east and were safely billeted in or near Kyoto. Ieyasu made his headquarters at Nijo Castle, Hidetada at Fushimi. The local *daimyo* had already been active. On 6 December Ikeda Toshitaka had made himself particularly useful by securing the rhomboidal island of rice fields called Nakajima that lay between the loop of the Yodogawa and the Nakatsugawa. It straddled one of the main roads north out of the castle, and enabled the Tokugawa lines in that area to be advanced to the north bank of the Tenmagawa.

Between 15 and 18 December Ieyasu and Hidetada made their way to Osaka from Kyoto. Ieyasu's plan was to set up field headquarters to the south of Osaka Castle, which involved the longest possible journey. Their approach was a cautious one, for more than military reasons. For simple considerations of safety the Tokugawa leaders travelled by way of Nara. This was a circuitous route, but a prudent one, because the approach was sheltered from the attentions of the Osaka garrison for almost the whole of its length by the bulk of the Ikoma mountains. The decision that any commander would then have had to make was where to turn west and cross the mountains. Ieyasu was going to use the Kuragari Pass, but someone remarked that there was a saying that no one ever won a victory after going over that pass. Thinking it sensible to humour the old superstition he avoided the pass and proceeded to Osaka by a road further to the south. As his generals were still busy securing positions close to the castle, Ieyasu and Hidetada set up temporary field headquarters some distance away. Ieyasu based himself at Sumiyoshi, Hidetada at Hirano.

Securing the riverside forts: 19–29 December 1614

On 19 December an important operation took place at the fort of Kizugawaguchi, which, as the name implies, lay at the mouth of the Kizugawa where it was joined by the Ikutama Canal. It was a vital strongpoint for Hideyori on the edge of the castle town, and was defended by Akashi Teruzumi. Hachisuka Yoshishige (1581–1615), who was to play a very active role during the Winter campaign, captured it for Ieyasu after fierce fighting, in which he was ably assisted by Asano Nagaakira (1586–1632), the lord of Wakayama Castle, and Ikeda Tadakatsu.

A few days later the focus of the Tokugawa operations shifted to the north-eastern edge of the castle's defences. The first action was conducted between the Hiranogawa and the Yamatogawa in the area called Shigino. Here too was a fort, and on 26 December Uesugi Kagekatsu captured it from Inoue Yoritsugu. The Osaka garrison then launched a fierce counterattack under Ono Harunaga, so Uesugi Kagekatsu had to be reinforced by Horio Tadaharu, Niwa Nagashige and Sakakibara Yasukatsu. On receiving reports of Kagekatsu's difficulties, Ieyasu suggested that he should pull back to rest his men and leave the proceedings to Horio Tadaharu. But this produced an indignant response from the veteran warrior, who told his master in no uncertain terms that he had been brought up never to retire once a fight had been started.

While this had been going on Satake Yoshinobu had been conducting a very similar operation within sight of Shigino, across the river to the north at a place called Imafuku. Here he captured three forts from Yano Masanori and Iida Iesada, but was then attacked by Kimura Shigenari and Goto Mototsugu, who left the castle by the Kyobashiguchi, crossed the bridge and fell on him from the west. But this counterattack was no more successful than the Shigino operation had been, and by the time night fell on 26 December these two key areas had been secured for Tokugawa Ieyasu.

The battle of Imafuku is also notable for an amusing incident that encapsulates the aesthetic side of the samurai life. The noted tea master Furuta Oribe Shigenari visited Satake Yoshinobu at Imafuku. Although less warlike than his kinsman Furuta Shigeharu (who was in the front line at the south of the castle and was to distinguish himself during the Summer campaign by taking 61 heads), Shigenari was at Imafuku in a totally military capacity. But when he noticed a barricade made from bamboo the tea master within him took over, and he felt himself unable to resist a brief inspection to see if any of the bamboo poles would make a good teaspoon. As he poked his head out a chance bullet struck him, at which he pulled out a purple napkin and nonchalantly wiped away the blood, 'as one would expect from a tea master', commented the onlookers. The next day found Shigenari in the presence of Ieyasu, to whom he showed off his 'war wound'. But Ieyasu had already been told the story of how it had been acquired, and was not greatly impressed.

Two final operations to secure the northern perimeter of Osaka Castle took place on 29 December. In the first, the battle of Bakuroguchi (otherwise Bakurogafuchi), Ishikawa Tadafusa (1572–1650) crossed the Kizugawa from the island of Ashijima to capture the fort of Bakuroguchi from Susukida Kanesuke. Hachisuka Yoshishige, who left his newly won position at Kizugawaguchi to attack Bakuroguchi from the south, assisted him. He was also unexpectedly assisted by the absence from the

The Sengan turret that flanks the entrance to Osaka Castle across the Oteguchi.

Satake Yoshinobu, one of the able generals who served Tokugawa Ieyasu at Osaka.

The battle of Imafuku. On the left the samurai of Satake Yoshinobu charge into action against Goto Mototsugu (black flags) and Kimura Shigenari (red flags). From a painted screen depicting the Winter campaign of Osaka in Osaka Castle Museum.

A two-storey gatehouse of Osaka Castle with a very solid set of gates.

scene of Susukida Kanesuke himself, who was lying drunk in a brothel while his fort was being captured.

A remarkable action took place that same day a little to the north. In the battle of Noda-Fukushima, Kuki Moritaka secured the estuary beside the Noda fort. Moritaka is an interesting character. He was the son of Kuki Yoshitaka (1542–1600), a reformed pirate whose naval expertise had been vital in securing Nobunaga's victory over the Ikko-ikki on that same estuary 40 years earlier. Yoshitaka had then become one of Hideyoshi's leading admirals during the Korean invasion, but ended up on the losing side at Sekigahara. His son Moritaka, however, served Ieyasu during that campaign and was well rewarded. The winter of 1614 saw him following in his father's footsteps as he took control of the naval arm during the siege of Osaka.

The Noda operation involved the use of a *mekura bune* (literally 'blind ship'), which was very similar to the *kobaya*, the smallest type of Japanese warship. Instead of the cloth curtains that were hung from the *kobaya*'s surrounding frame, 30cm (1ft) diameter bamboo bundles were suspended to give a light but absorbent protective screen all round. A pitched bamboo roof of similar construction lay along the boat. Four square holes were cut on each side, through which poked the barrels of eight *furanki* (European breech-loading swivel guns) with their mounting spikes sunk into the vertical posts of the *mekura bune*'s sides. Each gun had a crew of three men: a loader who dropped the breech container into the breech and forced a retaining wedge in behind it; the aimer, whose hands were on the wooden tiller added behind the breech; and the firer, who stood ready with a fuse on a short linstock. To make room for these eight guns and their crews the number of oars was cut back to 18 on each side. With the aid of the *mekura bune* the fort of Noda was bombarded and captured. Ikeda Tadatsugu (1599–1615), the brother of Toshitaka, then took the nearby fort of Fukushima by moving overland against the weakened defences.

The Toyotomi response: October–December 1614

Apart from the brave attempts to recapture the outlying forts that were described above, very little had been happening within the castle itself. To some extent, admittedly, there was not much need for Hideyori to do anything except sit and wait for the Tokugawa army to feel the pangs of hunger long before his well-supplied garrison began to suffer in that way. In fact, if the accounts are to be believed, Hideyori's attempts both to lead his men and to increase their morale seem to have been disastrous failures.

The details of the Tokugawa siege lines are shown here in a section from a painted screen depicting the Winter campaign of Osaka in Osaka Castle Museum. The planking of the bridge has been torn up, so Tokugawa *ashigaru* keep up a fire across the moat behind the protection of sandbags. To the right a mounted officer controls his troops, sheltered from defensive fire by bundles of green bamboo.

First, his mother, the redoubtable but somewhat naïve Yodogimi, thought that it would be a good way of rousing the spirits of the defenders if she dressed herself and four ladies-in-waiting in samurai armour and, thus attired, inspected the troops. The reaction to this apparition by the hard-bitten *ronin* may be imagined, but their conclusion – that women in armour meant that Osaka had a deficit of real leaders – seems to have been lost on their commander. Not long after this incident one of Hideyori's least inspiring generals, Oda Yorinaga, nephew of the great Nobunaga and son of Oda Yuraku (1548–1622), the celebrated tea master, tried a similar scheme himself. Clad in a fetching gold-lacquered armour, and accompanied by a comely wench similarly dressed, he toured the ramparts during the night and required his female attendant to spank any sentry caught asleep.

Hideyori aroused even less enthusiasm himself, because for some time he had no meetings with his generals at all. When it was suggested that such a course of action might be advantageous he consented to grant them an audience. The story, which may be apocryphal but sums up the relationship admirably, tells how they assembled in the main audience chamber of the castle's *yashiki*, and had their spirits raised by the arrival of the late Hideyoshi's golden gourd standard, the insignia under which they and their fathers had fought. Unfortunately, the arrival of Hideyoshi's son and heir had the opposite affect on their morale. He merely muttered words to the effect of 'Thank you for all your trouble', and left. Hideyori's generals were simply left to their own devices.

They certainly did their best, but in the absence of any aggressive strategy Osaka Castle was totally surrounded by the end of 1614. We may detect a note of sympathy towards Toyotomi Hideyori on behalf of the East India Company, because the account book of the EIC factory contains the following poignant entry for 28 December 1614:

> *Presents given:*
> *To 50* catties *Japan gunpowder,*
> *bought to give Fidaia Samma, Prince of Osaka* £17 5s 0d
> *A new hat given his secretary* £6 0s 0d

The battle of the Sanada maru: 3–4 January 1615

The battle of Noda-Fukushima had ensured that all the outlying forts of Osaka were now in the hands of Tokugawa Ieyasu, so his troops began settling in to the final siege lines shown on p.38. A virtual town grew up on all sides, where the samurai besiegers were accommodated in simple one-storey buildings roofed with thatch and defended against attack by wooden palisades. Open-work watchtowers were erected at regular intervals, and flags fluttered to show the adherence of the particular *daimyo* whose sector it was. Squads of *ashigaru* sharpshooters would creep forward along angled sap trenches until they were quite near to the river that provided the castle's outer moat. A mound of earth would be piled up in front to create a firing platform. On top of this, bundles of straw, made identically to rice bales but containing sand, were arranged to give an absorbent front parapet. From behind these the *ashigaru* kept up a constant fire against the defenders. In other places temporary barriers were provided by means of bundles of green bamboo, which had similar

The defensive additions made to Osaka Castle by Toyotomi Hideyori prior to the Winter campaign are shown in this model in Osaka Castle Museum. Walls have been added to the inside of the Ikutama Canal. They are fitted with an upper-level firing platform. Two simple towers with tiled roofs flank the gate. In case of a night attack illumination is provided by lanterns slung down to the water, where there are loose palisades.

One of the few areas of high ground to the south of Osaka Castle is the hill of Chausuyama. During the Winter campaign Chausuyama housed Ieyasu's field headquarters. During the Summer campaign it was occupied by Sanada Yukimura, and much fierce fighting took place around it.

projectile-absorbent properties. Large bundles would be rolled forwards by a team and then levered into a vertical position. A few heavy shields with their fronts protected by iron plates were also used. These shields had loopholes for firing.

Both Ieyasu and Hidetada now advanced their respective headquarters further towards the castle, choosing two of the only three hills that lay in front of Osaka. Ieyasu set up his golden fan standard on Chausuyama to the south of the Shitennoji Temple. Hidetada took charge at Okayama to the east. As usual, Ieyasu's field headquarters were characteristically modest: just a simple building similar to that of his samurai, but large enough to accommodate his generals for councils of war. When everyone was in place the first major attack on the defences of Osaka Castle began.

The target of attack – the only major assault in the whole of the Winter campaign – was the Sanada maru and the dry moat and wall that kept the Tokugawa away from the inner defences on the southern side. Sanada Yukimura had in fact set up a post somewhat in advance of the

Sanada Yukimura's statue stands on the site of the Sanada maru, the earthwork barbican that he successfully defended during the Winter campaign.

This detail from the painted screen depicting the Winter campaign of Osaka in Osaka Castle Museum shows the Tokugawa siege lines and the Osaka defensive lines opposite each other. The Osaka side has demolished all the bridges in this sector and have erected loose palisades inside the moat. The walls are very solid with loopholes, and illumination is provided by lanterns slung out across the moat on pulleys. The Tokugawa troops have dug themselves in, excavating earth mounds on top of which they have built barricades of sandbags. Bamboo bundles provide the other form of defence.

defensive position that bore his name. This was on Sasayama, the only unoccupied hill in front of the castle, but when he learned from his scouts that an attack was imminent he evacuated it for the safety of the lines. Sasayama was then occupied with a shout of triumph by the samurai of Maeda Toshitsune (1593–1658), son of the famous Toshiie, who had the distinction of being the wealthiest *daimyo* in Japan under the Tokugawa. Some of the Maeda unit continued their advance as far as the Sanada maru, and at daybreak a stream of insults from inside the fortifications had the expected results: Maeda Toshitsune's men tried to climb the walls, and Sanada Yukimura's men cut them down with arquebus fire. The Sanada maru, with its possibility of crossfire into the ditch, was a death trap.

Maeda Toshitsune was followed into the attack by Ieyasu's grandson Matsudaira Tadanao (1595–1650). He had displeased his grandfather by arriving somewhat late on the battlefield, but proceeded to redeem himself by leading his men down into the ditch and up the other side, where they were met by a hail of bullets from the defences. Accompanying him was Ii Naotaka (1590–1659), whose samurai stood out from the rest of the army because they were all dressed in the red-lacquered armour that gave them the nickname the 'red devils'. His illustrious father Ii Naomasa had died in 1602 and was succeeded by his incompetent son Naokatsu, even though he had wished that his illegitimate son Naotaka should take over the domain. In 1614, when the Osaka campaign was just beginning, Tokugawa Ieyasu took a hand in the family affairs and ordered Naotaka to lead the Ii contingent into battle.

Ii Naotaka had inherited his father Naomasa's territories and his red-clad samurai army, so it is not surprising to note the name of Miura Yo'emon in his service. He hailed from the province of Iga, and may therefore have had ninja connections, even if he was not an actual ninja himself. Ieyasu had presented him to Ii Naomasa in 1583. At the battle

of Sekigahara Ii Naomasa was wounded by a bullet in his elbow, and received first aid from Miura Yo'emon.

Miura Yo'emon was present with Ii Naotaka during the attack on the Sanada maru. Casualties were mounting, and a retreat was called, but because of the noisy mêlée the order was scarcely heard. Yo'emon, who was currently removing arrowheads from the wounded, ordered his ninja into action in a move that showed a subtle understanding of the samurai mind. They approached the mass of men in the moat and fired on them at random. Their comrades, surprised by the arrows that came flying at them from behind, turned towards them and thus 'attacked to safety', the need for an actual 'retreat' having been avoided.

Ii Naotaka and Matsudaira Tadanao then made an attack further along the southern wall to the gateway of Hachomeguchi, through which passed an important road. The entrance through the wall was protected by a *toraguchi* (tiger's mouth) gateway, set at an angle and requiring a 90-degree turn by an attacker, but the fury of their assault against the gate and the ramparts allowed them temporary entry into what was 'officially' Osaka Castle. They were the first of the Tokugawa samurai to do so, but their stay was a short one. Kimura Shigenari, the young general who was one of Hideyori's leading commanders, had charge of this sector and led a spirited counterattack that drove the easterners out. Shigenari then followed up this success by attacking other Tokugawa troops who had moved up in support. The names of their commanders are given as Terazawa Hirotaka (1563–1633) and Matsukura Shigemasa (1574–1630), both of whom hailed from the western side of Kyosho. His attack drove them back into the lines controlled by Matsudaira Tadanao, causing utter

The attack on the Hachomeguchi gateway by Matsudaira Tadanao, whose flags bear the 'Y' shaped device. This section from the painted screen depicting the Winter campaign of Osaka in Osaka Castle Museum shows the detail of the defences of the southern wall and the Sanada maru. The walls are made predominately of wood, with two levels of firing position.

Behind the Matsudaira samurai come the troops of Ii Naotaka, easily recognizable by their red armour and flags bearing the 'I' character. The breaching of the ramparts allowed them temporary entry into what was 'officially' Osaka Castle. They were the first of the Tokugawa samurai to enter, but their stay was a short one. From a painted screen depicting the Winter campaign of Osaka in Osaka Castle Museum.

confusion. The fighting lasted for several hours, at the end of which the Osaka troops withdrew, well satisfied with their day's work.

The following day, 4 January 1615, the Tokugawa side mounted an attack on the next gate along the wall towards the west. This was the Tanimachiguchi, and the assault was led by Todo Takatora (1556–1630), a veteran of the Korean campaign who had twice retired voluntarily to Koyasan and twice been recalled because his talents were sorely needed. His initial success in breaking through was helped by dissension among the defenders, who were under the command of Oda Nagayori, great-grandson of the famous Nobunaga. But just as on the previous day, no sooner had they forced their way into the extended castle grounds than they were subjected to a lively counterattack that drove them out again. In this case it was delivered by Chosokabe Morichika. Todo Takatora's *hata bugyo* (commissioner for flags) played a vital part in rallying the retreating army, as the following account from *Shahon Heiyo Roku* tells us:

> At the time of the Winter campaign of Osaka, when Todo Izumi no kami's vanguard were routed, the Todo family's hata bugyo Kuki Shirobei hoisted three out of the flags he was entrusted with, and stepped forward into the middle of the fleeing men. He set up the flags where they could be seen, and Shirobei knelt down, with the flags in front of the vanguard standing firm, and the soldiers who had been retreating were encouraged by this and came to a halt. Soon they turned back, dressed their ranks, and were again fighting men.

The experience of the two days was a sobering one for Ieyasu. Hidetada had been in favour of launching an all-out assault on the castle, but he soon changed his tune. The three failures at the southern wall, which was after all only a comparatively rudimentary structure, confirmed the worst fears of his experienced father that no attack on such a huge and well-defended castle was likely to succeed. Something else was needed.

The attack on the Tanimachiguchi is led by Todo Takatora, whose heraldic device is three white discs on black. He is followed by Terazawa Hirotaka (three black discs on white). From the painted screen depicting the Winter campaign in Osaka Castle Museum.

THE ARTILLERY BOMBARDMENT

The failure of the attack on the Sanada maru led Ieyasu to deploy his 'secret weapon' against Osaka, because the one area in which the Tokugawa had a real advantage over the defenders lay in their possession of modern long-range artillery.

The Tokugawa artillery

Tokugawa Ieyasu had obtained his artillery from the English and Dutch traders. The first mention of English cannon being sold occurs in a letter from Richard Wickham in Edo to William Eaton in Osaka of 4 July 1614, where there is a brief mention that 'Captain Adams hath made sale of the ordnance and munitions'. Wickham's sole concern here is the fact that Adams has not yet been paid, but on the same day he writes to Cocks in Hirado mentioning ordnance, powder, shot and lead, all of which are 'well sold'. Once again the description is tantalizingly brief, but a precise identification for the cannon and their origin may be found in the report submitted by Richard Cocks to the EIC in London, dated 5 December 1614. Tokugawa Ieyasu had bought four culverins and one saker, and all five guns had been brought to Japan on board the *Clove*:

> *The Emperor took the 4 culverins & one saker for one thousand four hundred* tays *and ten barrels of powder at one hundred eighty and four* tays *and 600 bars of lead…*

Culverins fired shot of 8kg (17 1/2lb) while the smaller sakers fired shot of 2.5kg (5 1/2lb). That these weapons were carried for trade and were not part of the *Clove*'s own armaments is confirmed by an earlier letter from Cocks to Wickham of January 1614, where they are listed among other cargo items as 'five pieces ordnance… £35 8s 4d.'

The use of the four English culverins and one saker appears in Japanese accounts of the siege of Osaka. They made up half of Tokugawa

THE ATTACK ON THE HACHOMEGUCHI GATEWAY DURING THE WINTER CAMPAIGN, 3 JANUARY 1615 (pages 50–51)

In preparation for the siege of Osaka Castle Toyotomi Hideyori ordered that a dry moat should be cut across the vulnerable southern side of the castle to link the Nekomagawa and the Ikutama Canal. The new defences consisted of a wooden palisade (1) on top of an earthwork made from the excavation of a dry ditch (2), strengthened at its eastern end by a barbican known as the Sanada maru. The wall was rough-plastered and fitted with loopholes and towers (3). Certain key roads from Osaka passed through the wall, and at these points gateways were built, protected by a right-angled turn within the wall. On 3 January 1615, after an unsuccessful attempt against the Sanada maru, the Tokugawa army launched an attack against the Hachomeguchi gateway. They broke through into what

was 'officially' Osaka Castle, but their stay was a short one. Kimura Shigenari, the young general who was one of Hideyori's leading commanders, had charge of this sector and led a spirited counter-attack that drove them out. Shigenari then followed up this success by attacking other Tokugawa troops who had moved up in support. In this plate we are down in the ditch with Matsudaira Tadanao (1595–1650), Tokugawa Ieyasu's grandson (4). He wears an elaborate embossed suit of armour (5). His samurai are identified by the white 'y' device on their black flags (6). His long *nobori* banners bear the 'y' in black on white (7). Some of the flags are carried on the backs of *ashigaru* in specially strengthened pouches, as shown by the man falling to his death (8). Other *ashigaru* try to keep up a covering fire on the slippery slope (9), but they are easy targets for the *ashigaru* of the Osaka garrison, who rain fire down upon them from the parapet (10). (Richard Hook)

While their comrades to the rear march into action, a group of *ashigaru* enjoys a bowl of rice brought by one of the towns-people. To their left one *ashigaru* has a final drag on his pipe.

The Shibatsuji gun is Japan's oldest cannon. It was named after its maker Shibatsuji Ryuemon Sukenobu and was made in 1614. It is 3.27m (10ft 8in) in overall length with a surprisingly small bore of 90mm (3.5in). This was the only true Japanese-made siege cannon deployed during the Osaka campaign, and is now on show in the Yushukan Museum in the Yasukuni Shrine in Tokyo.

Ieyasu's complement of European heavy cannon, because other sources state that Tokugawa Ieyasu also had five *ishibiya* obtained from the Dutch. *Ishibiya* was the term used later in Japan to refer specifically to cannon firing a shot of one *kanme* or more. The smaller of the Dutch weapons could fire shot of one *kanme* 500 *monme* (5.6kg or about 12lb), while the larger weapon fired a shot of between four and five *kanme* (16–18.8kg or 35–40lb). A different Japanese source says that Ieyasu obtained 12 *ishibiya* from the Dutch, but that it is not clear how many of them were heavy breech-loaders or smaller muzzle loaders.

By comparison with the detailed records of the sale of the English guns to the Tokugawa, the numbers, weights and source of supply of the five Dutch cannon remains a mystery. There appear to be no records of Dutch ships selling either trade guns or their own armaments in the months immediately prior to the siege of Osaka, so the most likely source is the cargo of the ill-fated *Liefde* in 1600. It was noted earlier that Ieyasu confiscated her cannon, variously counted as either 18 or 26 in number.

Tokugawa Ieyasu's ten European cannon dwarfed the Japanese guns he possessed both in size and power, even though they comprised only ten of the 300 pieces that he finally deployed around Osaka Castle. Prior to Osaka, Ieyasu had bought up all the cannon he could lay his hands on, and this included commissioning from the arsenal in Sakai a specimen that is now the oldest surviving Japanese cannon. It is known as the Shibatsuji gun, from its maker Shibatsuji Ryuemon Sukenobu. It was made in 1614, and is 3.27m (10ft 8in) in overall length with a bore of 90mm (3.5in). The Yasukuni Shrine museum estimates the weight of the shot it fired as one *kanme* 500 *monme*, which is similar to that fired by the smaller sizes of Dutch cannon. There may have been other heavy Japanese guns cast, but none has survived. Ieyasu hunted far and wide to collect both cannon and arquebuses, and obtained weapons from many sources in addition to the well-established Japanese gunmakers at Sakai and

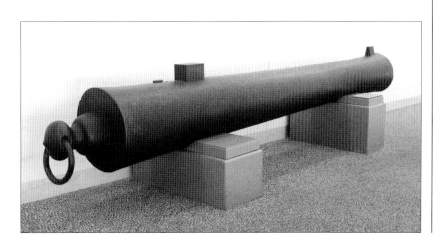

THE NIGHT ATTACK ACROSS THE HONMACHI BRIDGE BY BAN NAOTSUGU, 16 JANUARY 1615 (pages 54–55)

On the night of 16 January 1615, the Tokugawa received an unexpected response to their artillery bombardment of Osaka Castle. Ban Naotsugu, whose sector covered the Honmachi bridge leading to the west, launched a surprise attack across the bridge against the siege lines of Hachisuka Yoshishige. They returned with many heads and greatly increased morale. In this plate we see the details of the defences across a typical Osaka moat. The simple wooden walls are fitted with an upper-level firing platform. Two simple towers with tiled roofs flank the gate (1). Illumination is provided by paper lanterns slung on ropes and pulleys (2). Their weak light extends to the water, where there are loose palisades protruding from the surface (3). The central section of the railings of the bridge has been removed as a defence, and this has caused many casualties (4). Ban Naotsugu, identified by his name on his *sashimono* (5), leads his men on horseback. His samurai have red *sashimono* (6), as their identification. They are conducting a fierce hand-to-hand struggle against the samurai of Hachisuka Yoshishige, whose long *nobori* flags bear the *mon* of a black swastika (an ancient Buddhist symbol) against a black and white background (7). It has a little flag attached to it (8). One of the Hachisuka men in a red suit of armour falls to his death into the moat (9). Another tumbles off on the far side (10). (Richard Hook)

A full-sized reproduction of a Portuguese *furanki* (breech-loading cannon) at the castle of Usuki. These weapons were the mainstay of Hideyori's defensive artillery, and were no match for Tokugawa Ieyasu's muzzle-loading culverins and sakers.

Kunitomo. Many were 50 *monme* pieces, delivering only half the weight of shot of the lowest category of Japanese cannon (*ozutsu*). Such guns were essentially heavy arquebuses that were supported on a wall and had a serpentine rather than a touch-hole. They had a maximum range of between 1,500 and 1,600m (4,921 and 5,249ft). One, which is 3m (9ft 10in) long and 'the longest gun in Japan', is illustrated in the book by Yoshioka. It was made in 1610 and was used by the Tokugawa side at Osaka.

Hideyori's artillery

Apart from the Shibatsuji gun, therefore, all of Ieyasu's heavy cannon were of European manufacture. The Dutch and English cannon were the most important, but he may also have had several smaller breech-loaders – the type of cannon that made up Hideyori's total defensive arsenal. Richard Cocks noted in 1617 that the Japanese were 'better used to ordnance that hath chambers than whole pieces', and these types, known as *furanki,* had been the usual form of cannon seen in Japan prior to the arrival of the Dutch in 1600. Hideyori's *furanki* may have been Portuguese originals or, more likely, cast under Portuguese supervision at Nagasaki or Goa. Like the smaller specimens used on board Kuki Moritaka's *mekura bune,* they were mounted on a swivel and loaded by means of a removable chamber shaped rather like a beer mug, which was held in place by a hammered wooden wedge. Leakage round the breech meant a reduced muzzle velocity compared to muzzle-loading cannon, but this was somewhat compensated for by the speed of reloading, as additional chambers could be made ready. An extant specimen used by the Otomo family in 1586 has an overall length of 2.88m (9ft 5in) and a bore of 95mm (3.74in), which is similar to the Shibatsuji gun. The Toyotomi side had two large *furanki* of this size that were mounted on either side of the Sakura gate and were named 'Taro' and 'Jiro'. They fired shot of one *kanme* – similar to the Shibatsuji gun, but totally outclassed by Ieyasu's purchases. The fact that Osaka 'bristled with guns' belied their relative ineffectiveness.

The map on p.38 includes annotations that show where and how both sides deployed their cannon. The Tokugawa placed long-range weapons in the sections of the lines to the south of the castle controlled by Ii Naotaka, Todo Takatora and Matsudaira Tadanao, from where the Toyotomi defences could be easily reached by the culverins. Positions to the north of the castle were more useful for targeting the keep, and included the island of Bizenjima, 750m (2,460ft) from the keep, from where guns fired across two rivers and two moats. These positions had been secured by the Tokugawa side as a result of the operations late in 1614. The Toyotomi side simply dispersed their cannon round the walls, but even Taro and Jiro were out of range of the Tokugawa lines.

The bombardment of Osaka Castle: 8–19 January 1615

After a consultation with his senior advisers, Ieyasu ordered a limited bombardment of Osaka Castle to begin on 8 January 1615. It was carried out for three consecutive days at ten o'clock at night and at dawn. Meanwhile, miners began tunnelling under the walls. Messages calling upon the defenders to surrender were fired into the castle by arrow, but none produced any response.

When the full bombardment of Osaka Castle began on 15 January the Tokugawa cannon provided a unique and terrifying phenomenon unknown in Japan up to that moment. A nobleman in Kyoto noted in his diary that the sound of firing could be heard from there, and the psychological effects on the defenders of the castle soon proved to be far more important than any actual structural damage. This must have been Ieyasu's intention right from the start. Not only did he have no more than ten heavy cannon with which to bombard a fortress that had outer walls nearly 14.5km (9 miles) in circumference, but the construction of Japanese castle walls, which were massive stone bases with a solid earth core, were invulnerable to any contemporary artillery. In 1945 the stone base of Hiroshima Castle even withstood the atomic bomb. To add to the psychological pressure, Ieyasu ordered that at certain times during the night volleys of arquebus fire should be let off and great war cries raised, so that the defenders would believe that an attack was imminent.

The fight within the Tokugawa lines that followed the night attack across the Honmachi bridge led by Ban Naotsugu. From the painted screen depicting the Winter campaign in Osaka Castle Museum.

It took just one day for these tactics to yield a response, but it was by no means what Ieyasu had been anticipating. On the night of 16 January Ban Naotsugu, whose sector covered the Honmachi bridge on the western perimeter, launched a surprise assault. Lit only by the moon and by the lanterns slung out across the river on pulleys, Naotsugu's samurai charged over the bridge and into the nearest Tokugawa contingent, which happened to be that of Hachisuka Yoshishige. The Osaka troops took many heads before retiring.

The bombardment continued, and even though there was no prospect of levelling the stone walls, Osaka, like all Japanese castles, also consisted of elaborate superstructures made of wood that were raised on top of the stone bases to provide accommodation, storage and defensive areas. The range of the European cannon meant that these buildings, normally untouched until the final assault on a castle, could be attacked from the Tokugawa lines. The tactics began to achieve results on 15 January 1615, when one cannon, deliberately targeted onto the apartments used by Hideyori's mother Yodogimi, succeeded in dropping a cannonball onto the tea cabinet she was using at the time. This event caused great alarm to the lady who was a key opinion-leader (to put it mildly) among the Osaka hierarchy.

On 17 January, the anniversary of Hideyoshi's death, the Tokugawa side calculated that, as his dutiful son and heir, Hideyori would visit his father's shrine in the castle. A cannon was fired when they considered that the time was right. The shot missed Hideyori, but struck his mother's apartments again. This time the cannon ball took out a wooden pillar, which crushed to death two of her ladies-in-waiting. Yodogimi was terrified. As the late Hideyoshi's widow, she exerted a considerable influence over her son, and the most decisive result of the Tokugawa bombardment was to bring the Toyotomi side to the negotiation table.

THE PEACE NEGOTIATIONS

Ieyasu had already made offers to Hideyori through third parties, promising a free pardon to all the *ronin* and giving Hideyori two provinces in place of Osaka. As the provinces on offer were two in which Hideyori could be completely controlled by the Tokugawa, Hideyori had countered with a demand for two provinces on Shikoku island, but that was unacceptable to Ieyasu.

Negotiations were conducted with Yodogimi by Ieyasu's chief lady-in-waiting, Ocha no tsubone, who was a close friend of Yodogimi's sister. Ieyasu seems to have understood Yodogimi's mood perfectly, because she began to plead with her son for a settlement. The Osaka commanders scorned such a craven attitude. Goto Mototsugu emphasized the need for resistance and unity, and even Hideyori rose to the occasion, stating that he was prepared to make the castle his tomb. Goto Mototsugu also suggested, to deaf ears, that Sanada Yukimura should be put in supreme command of the castle.

The Osaka generals may have disagreed about tactics, but they all agreed on one thing: that Tokugawa Ieyasu could not be trusted. Some may have been aware of the story of how he had reached a peace settlement with the Ikko-ikki armies in his native Mikawa province almost half a century before. One of the clauses in the agreement was that the temples should be restored to their original state. Ieyasu had them all burned down, arguing that green fields was their natural state.

Yet there were others among the Osaka leaders who saw in a settlement with the Tokugawa the best hopes of regaining what they had lost. Ocha no tsubone went to and fro with offer and counter-offer. Perhaps Hideyori would be allowed to retain the castle? Perhaps hostages would be exchanged? Perhaps the ramparts should be levelled and the moat filled in? All these offers and suggestions were reported to Yodogimi, who heard more clearly, and much louder, the sound of the English culverins. Then one day it was reported back to Ieyasu that Yodogimi was 'overjoyed' that a satisfactory conclusion had been reached. The final document of surrender, for that was what it was, was fittingly sealed by Ieyasu with blood from his finger. It stated that the *ronin* inside the castle were not to be held to account, that Hideyori's revenue should remain what it was and that he and Yodogimi could choose freely where they wanted to live.

This all happened on 21 January 1615. Ieyasu made a great show about ordering his men to stand down, and on the following day thousands of them put down their swords and took up pickaxes and shovels, and began to demolish Osaka Castle's outer wall. The rubble thus produced was tossed into the moat. Needless to say Ono Harunaga, the Osaka commander who was first on the scene, protested that this had not been in the peace agreement, but his complaints only served to make Ieyasu's demolition squads work that much harder. When Yodogimi was told, she was furious, and lodged a protest at the highest level, but Ieyasu was already on his way back to Kyoto. Meanwhile the destruction of Osaka's outer defensive line proceeded with great rapidity, and was almost complete by the time Hideyori's complaints were officially answered. The Tokugawa response was dismissive, and made the point, as if to a small child, that as eternal peace had now been established there was no need for a wall anyway.

The work of filling in the moats was conducted under the direct supervision of the Shogun Tokugawa Hidetada, whom Ieyasu had left in charge. On 28 January Ieyasu was formally received in audience by the emperor of Japan, to whom he passed on the wonderful news of the peaceful conclusion of the Winter campaign of Osaka. On 8 February Ieyasu commissioned cannon from the gunsmiths of Kunitomo. The Summer campaign had already begun.

THE SUMMER CAMPAIGN

OPPOSING PLANS

The Summer campaign of Osaka was one of the most dramatic and decisive events in Japanese history. The latter feature, its decisiveness, was certainly included in the plans that Tokugawa Ieyasu had been carefully laying even while the Winter campaign was still in progress. The former feature, that of drama, surprises and quick decisions having to be made in the face of sudden reverses of fortune, was definitely not on his agenda.

Tokugawa Ieyasu's plans

All the evidence points to a belief on Ieyasu's part that the weakened castle was now at his mercy. He probably did not think that it would be an easy victory, but he clearly believed that the Summer campaign would begin where the Winter campaign had left off. Ieyasu therefore planned to use Chausuyama and Okayama once again as the joint Tokugawa headquarters, but, to his great surprise, neither he nor his son got near to either place. Instead of the planned creation of siege lines, a bombardment from much closer range and a final assault on the castle after an appropriate wait, the Summer campaign developed rapidly into something that the Winter campaign had never been. It became a war of movement with almost none of the characteristics of a siege. Furthermore, in contrast to the long slog of the Winter campaign, it was all over in a few days, and the Tokugawa side nearly lost.

Toyotomi Hideyori's plans

It was noted earlier that prior to the Winter campaign Hideyori's ablest generals had planned to stall the Tokugawa advance by occupying Kyoto and securing the passes through the Ikoma mountains. The scheme was never carried out, but when the Tokugawa faced him during the summer with a new advance against his weakened castle, Hideyori had little choice but to risk a similar pre-emptive operation. The winter plans were therefore put into operation, although on a much-reduced scale. Seizing Kyoto and Seta was out of the question, so the greatest generals on the Osaka side planned to stop the Tokugawa army while it was on its way from Kyoto to the castle. The movements of the massive Tokugawa army could not be kept secret, so once it was clear which roads its men had chosen, it would be time to move out and stop them. The Summer campaign, therefore, began with an operation away from Osaka in a way never seen during the Winter campaign. Taken out of context, the plan looks like a do-or-die sally out of the castle. In reality it was Hideyori's best hope; the castle was seriously weakened, and attack had to be the best means of defence. Hideyori had very little choice in the matter.

SUMMER CAMPAIGN OF OSAKA

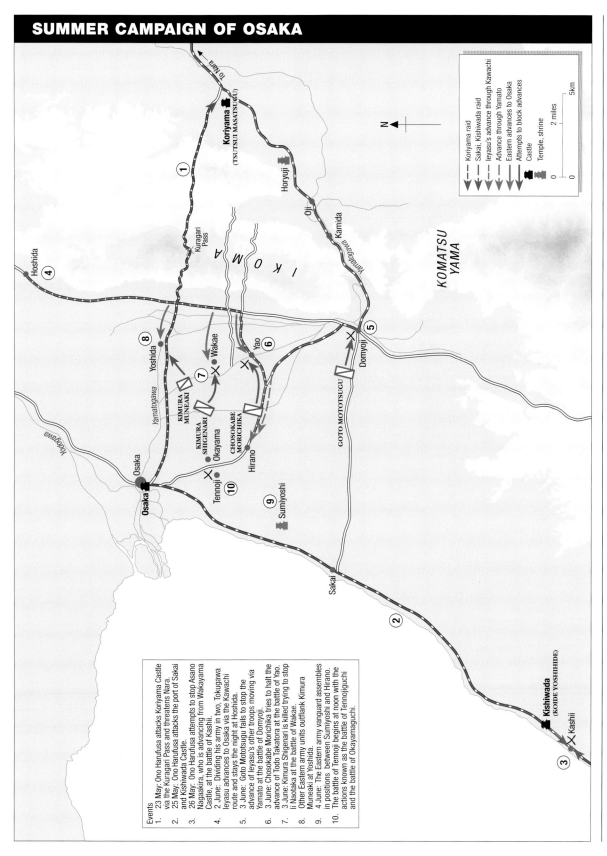

Events

1. 23 May: Ono Harufusa attacks Koriyama Castle via the Kuragari Pass and threatens Nara.
2. 25 May: Ono Harufusa attacks the port of Sakai and Kishiwada Castle.
3. 26 May: Ono Harufusa attempts to stop Asano Nagaakira, who is advancing from Wakayama Castle, at the battle of Kashii.
4. 2 June: Dividing his army in two, Tokugawa Ieyasu advances to Osaka via the Kawachi route and stays the night at Hoshida.
5. 3 June: Goto Mototsugu fails to stop the advance of Ieyasu's other troops moving via Yamato at the battle of Domyoji.
6. 3 June: Chosokabe Morichika tries to halt the advance of Todo Takatora at the battle of Yao.
7. 3 June: Kimura Shigenari is killed trying to stop Ii Naotaka at the battle of Wakae.
8. Other Eastern army units outflank Kimura Muneaki at Yoshida.
9. 4 June: The Eastern army vanguard assembles in positions between Sumiyoshi and Hirano. The battle of Tennoji begins at noon with the actions known as the battle of Tennojiguchi and the battle of Okayamaguchi.
10. The battle of Tennoji begins at noon with the actions known as the battle of Tennojiguchi and the battle of Okayamaguchi.

63

One of the famous 'big stones' of Osaka Castle, with the author providing the comparison. In fact these great stones are not quite as impressive as they look when it is discovered that the apparently massive blocks are a mere 60cm (2ft) thick.

ORDERS OF BATTLE

Eastern army

The best estimate for the Tokugawa army during the Summer campaign is between 150,000 and 160,000 men.

Tokugawa Ieyasu	30,000
Tokugawa Hidetada	20,000
Tokugawa Yoshinao	(included under Hidetada)
Tokugawa Yorinobu	(included under Hidetada)
Maeda Toshitsune	15,000
Katagiri Katsumoto	1,000
Hosokawa Tadaoki	3,500
Sanada Nobuyoshi	2,300
Honda Tadatomo	1,000
Asano Nagashige	1,000
Akita Sansue	1,000
Ogasawara Hidemasa	1,600
Hoshina Masamitsu	600
Sakakibara Yasukatsu	2,000
Suwa Tadazumi	540
Sengoku Tadamasa	1,000
Sakai Ietsugu	1,000
Matsudaira Yasunaga	600
Naito Tadaoki	600
Matsudaira Tadanao	10,000
Mizuno Katsushige	600
Honda Tadamasa	2,000
Matsudaira Tadaaki	1,000
Hitotsuyanagi Naomori	1,000
Tokunaga Masashige	1,200
Date Masamune	10,000
Murakami Yoshiaki	1,800
Tokugawa Tadateru	9,000
Mizoguchi Nobukatsu	1,000
Asano Nagaakira	5,000
Ikeda Tadatsugu	8,800
Kyogoku Tadataka	2,000

Kyogoku Takatomo	2,000
Ishikawa Tadafusa	2,300
Todo Takatora	5,000
Ii Naotaka	3,200
Hori Naoyori	600
Furuta Shigeharu	1,000
Mizoguchi Nobukatsu	1,000
Matsushita Shigetsuna	200
Matsukura Shigemasa	200
Okuda Tadatsugu	60
Niwa Ujinobu	200

The walls of Osaka Castle across the north outer moat.

Osaka army

Estimates for the number of men on the Osaka side during the Summer campaign vary widely owing to the unknown number of *ronin*. The Osaka army may have consisted of between 60,000 and 120,000 men.

Toyotomi Hideyori	3,080
Sanada Yukimura	3,500 (3,000 at Domyoji)
Kimura Shigenari	4,700
Kimura Muneaki	(included under Shigenari)
Yamaguchi Hirosada	500
Naito Sadatori	500
Miura Muneaki	300
Chosokabe Morichika	5,000
Mashita Moritsugu	300
Goto Mototsugu	2,800
Susukida Kanesuke	400
Inoue Tokitori	300
Akashi Morishige	2,000
Akashi Teruzumi	2,000
Asai Nagafusa	3,000
Yamaguchi Hirosada	500
Mori Katsunaga	4,000 (3,000 at Domyoji)
Yamagawa Katanobu	300
Kitagawa Nobukatsu	300
Yamamoto Kimio	200

Makishima Shigetoshi	200
Miyata Tokisada	2,000
Ono Harufusa	4,000 (3,000 at Kashii)
Ono Harunaga	5,000
Nagaoka Masachika	300
Otani Yoshihisa	2,000 (1,000 at Domyoji)
Fukushima Sadauji	2,500 (1,000 at Domyoji)
Watanabe Tadasu	500
Ogura Yukiharu	300

Leaders of *ronin*, and samurai serving in a personal capacity, with only a few personal retainers, included:

Okabe Noritsune
Ehara Takatsugu
Yoshida Yoshikore
Shingo Yukitomo
Takeda Eio
Fuse Den'emon

THE ADVANCE TO OSAKA

The pretext for Ieyasu's move against Osaka Castle in 1614 had been the notorious wording on the fateful temple bell. It was obvious that in 1615 no such excuse was likely to be offered to enable Ieyasu to return to the fray and proclaim that it was a just war; but a pretext did emerge, and it was every bit as ridiculous. What enraged Ieyasu in 1615 was a series of disturbing reports that he began receiving. Toyotomi Hideyori, whom he had spared and who had promised to live peacefully, had begun re-excavating the moats that the Tokugawa had taken such trouble to fill in. Not only that, but the *ronin*, to whom safe conduct had been so generously offered, had started to return to Osaka Castle.

Needless to say, both courses of action had been forced upon Toyotomi Hideyori because of reports he was receiving of the true intentions of Tokugawa Ieyasu. People had also begun to evacuate Kyoto because of rumours that the Osaka forces intended to seize the capital, and the wave of panic that swept through the region claimed the life of at least one innocent victim. This was the renowned tea master Furuta Oribe Shigenari, who was put to death with his son on suspicion of being involved in a plot to set fire to Kyoto and secure possession of the emperor. As this Shigenari was the elegant aesthete who had received a stray bullet at Imafuku for purely artistic reasons, the level of tension in the capital can be readily appreciated.

The Tokugawa advance from Edo to Kyoto: 1–22 May 1615
Tokugawa Ieyasu left Sumpu for the last campaign of his life on 1 May 1615. He was not officially off to war. The reason for his grand progress eastwards was to attend the wedding of his son Yoshinao in Nagoya Castle. The wedding was held, and no doubt a good time was had by all, but while Ieyasu was on his way at the head of a rather large and well-armed band of well-wishers, his son the Shogun sent out an order for all the loyal *daimyo* to assemble at Fushimi Castle. Hidetada left Edo on 7 May. With the nuptial celebrations completed, Ieyasu left Nagoya, but did not return to Sumpu. Instead he arrived in Nijo Castle on 15 May.

Hidetada joined him at nearby Fushimi on 18 May. Four days later the *daimyo*, who had by now assembled in accordance with their lord's commands, were ordered to march against Osaka Castle.

The Osaka raids and the final Tokugawa advance: 23–26 May 1615

It was on the following day, 23 May, that the Osaka generals began the forward strategy outlined above. The first to take the initiative was Ono Harufusa. Reasoning that the Tokugawa army, or at least part of it, would approach by the Nara road, Harufusa, accompanied by Goto Mototsugu, headed east over the Ikoma mountains on a raid. With complete disregard for the superstition that anyone who crossed the Kuragari Pass would lose a battle, Harufusa chose this direct route, and attacked Koriyama Castle, which was held for the Tokugawa by Tsutsui Masatsugu. The castle held out against them, so they returned to Osaka via Oji, burning the villages of Kamida and Horyoji on the way, but fortunately sparing the great Horyoji Temple, which remains to this day as the oldest wooden building in the world.

The following day Ono Harufusa set out again. This time he headed south along the coast of Osaka Bay, where the port of Sakai was the first place to feel his anger. He set fire to the town and then headed on towards the castle of Kishiwada, held for the Tokugawa by Koide Yoshihide. But some distance further on lay the very important castle of Wakayama, from where Asano Nagaakira was making ready to leave with 5,000 men as his contribution towards the Summer campaign. The two armies met at the battle of Kashii on 26 May. Ono Harufusa was defeated and withdrew to Osaka, leaving dead on the battlefield the first of many notable victims of the Summer campaign. This was Ban Naotsugu, the hero of the night attack across the Honmachi bridge.

On 2 June Ieyasu and Hidetada left Kyoto at the head of the Tokugawa army. We are told that Ieyasu rode in a palanquin, unarmoured, wearing a white kimono and a tea-coloured *haori* (jacket). The route he chose is interesting. His army marched in two divisions: the smaller part, consisting

The keep of Wakayama Castle, held for the Tokugawa by Asano Nagaakira. It was from Wakayama that Asano Nagaakira marched and took part in the battle of Kashii, one of the important preliminary skirmishes that made up the Summer campaign of Osaka.

of 38,000 men under Date Masamune and others, took the longer route through Nara on the far side of the Ikoma mountains; the larger section of 121,000 samurai under the Tokugawa father and son moved south on the near side of the Ikoma range, but for protection they travelled on a road that hugged the sides of the mountains. They stayed the night of 2 June at Hoshida, while the eastern contingent continued on its way, and ended up fighting one of the classic battles of Japanese history.

The battle of Domyoji, 'the battle among the tombs': 3 June 1615

If the battle of Domyoji had stood on its own it would undoubtedly be reckoned to be one of the great encounters in samurai history. Coming as it did the day before the battle of Tennoji it is inevitably overshadowed by that decisive struggle. But it is nonetheless remarkable in its own right for its location, if nothing else, because Domyoji was fought around and beside some of Japan's finest *kofun*, the enormous keyhole-shaped tombs that are the burial places of Japan's ancient emperors. These mysterious artificial mountains, usually enclosed by moats, date back to the first few centuries AD. Some of them are larger than the pyramids of ancient Egypt, but none has been excavated, for which the official reason given is that this would show disrespect to the ancestors of the imperial family. *Kofun* are dotted around the area of modern Nara Prefecture, and this particular corner of Japan, near the village of Domyoji, has several fine specimens. Among them is the tomb of Emperor Ojin, who was deified as Hachiman, the *kami* (deity) of war. What better place could there be for a battlefield?

Goto Mototsugu, however, had no intention of fighting a battle under the shadow of the imperial tombs. His 2,800 samurai were the vanguard of quite a large Osaka army, and his mission on 3 June 1615 was to secure the heights of Komatsuyama a little to the east. Komatsuyama lay just south of the Yamatogawa where it emerged through the only low-lying gap in the Ikoma mountain range. This was the route along which the eastern division of the Tokugawa army was heading. From Komatsuyama Goto Mototsugu could fall on them as they emerged through the pass.

The site of the battle of Domyoji, looking north towards the Ikoma mountains along the line of the channelled Ishikawa.

A single combat between Goto Mototsugu and Okubo Tadanori of the Tokugawa side, as depicted in a woodblock print by Yoshitoshi.

The well-tended grave of Susukida Kanesuke at Domyoji. Kanesuke disgraced himself during the Winter campaign for being found drunk in a brothel while his fort of Bakuroguchi was being captured. He redeemed himself by his exemplary conduct at the battle of Domyoji, where he was killed.

Just before Domyoji the Yamatogawa was joined by the Ishikawa, and then flowed northwards. In 1673 its direction was changed, and it now flows due west. The rivers around Domyoji have also been tamed, but there is still the same area of flatland set off by the striking *kofun*. In the early hours of the morning Goto Mototsugu forded the Ishikawa and approached Komatsuyama. As a sensible and experienced general he had sent out scouts, who reported to him that the Tokugawa army had already arrived at the pass, and were sending detachments up the eastern slopes of Komatsuyama. As dawn broke, and night was replaced by a dense fog, Mototsugu ordered an immediate charge up the western side, and the forces clashed on the top of the wooded mountain. At first Mototsugu's samurai began to drive the Tokugawa forces under Honda

OSAKA ARMY

1	Goto Mototsugu
2	Susukida Kanesuke
3	Yamamoto Kimio
4	Inoue Tokitoshi
5	Makishima Shigetoshi
6	Sanada Yukimura
7	Kitagawa Nobukatsu
8	Yamagawa Katanobu
9	Akashi Morishige
10	Fukushima Masamori
11	Watanabe Tadasu
12	Ogura Yukiharu
13	Otani Yoshihisa
14	Nagaoka Masachika
15	Igi Tokatsu
16	Miyata Tokisada
17	Mori Katsunaga

EASTERN ARMY

A	Mizuno Katsushige
B	Honda Tadamasa
C	Matsudaira Tadaaki
D	Date Masamune
E	Murakami Yoshiaki
F	Tokugawa Tadateru
G	Mizoguchi Nobukatsu

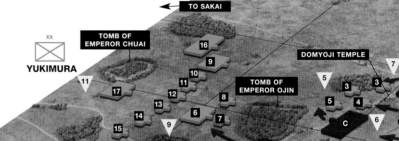

▼ EVENTS

1. **Goto Mototsugu crosses the ford on the Ishikawa River to secure the heights of Komatsuyama, but his scouts report Eastern army units advancing up the eastern slope of Komatsuyama.**

2. **4.00AM Goto Mototsugu charges up Komatsuyama and begins to push the Eastern army back.**

3. **5.00AM In response to a fierce counter-attack Goto withdraws to the summit of Komatsu to await reinforcements, who are delayed by dense fog. Fierce fighting continues.**

4. **10.00AM Goto Mototsugu is shot and commits *seppuku*. His army is overwhelmed.**

5. **10.00AM Fog clears to reveal that the Osaka army have reached the vicinity of the imperial tombs to the west of the Ishikawa River near the village of Domyoji.**

6. **The advance units of the Eastern army ford the river and engage the left wing of the Osaka army in the vicinity of the ancient imperial tombs.**

7. **Susukida Kanesuke is killed during this engagement.**

8. **12.00PM Sanada Yukimura engages Date Masamune in battle near the Konda Hachiman Shrine.**

9. **5.00PM Sanada Yukimura begins a retreat.**

10. **Tokuwaga Tadateru is ordered to pursue Sanada, but refuses.**

11. **The survivors of the Osaka army withdraw.**

THE BATTLE OF DOMYOJI, 3 JUNE 1615

Otherwise known as the 'battle among the tombs', Domyoji was fought around and beside some of Japan's finest kofun, the enormous keyhole-shaped tombs that are the burial places of Japan's ancient emperors. Goto Mototsugu and his 2,800 samurai, aimed to secure the heights of Komatsuyama a little to the east, and there ambush the eastern division of the Tokugawa army. Heavy fog impeded the Osaka army and the battle ended with heavy losses on both sides.

Note: Gridlines are shown at intervals of 1km (1093 yds)

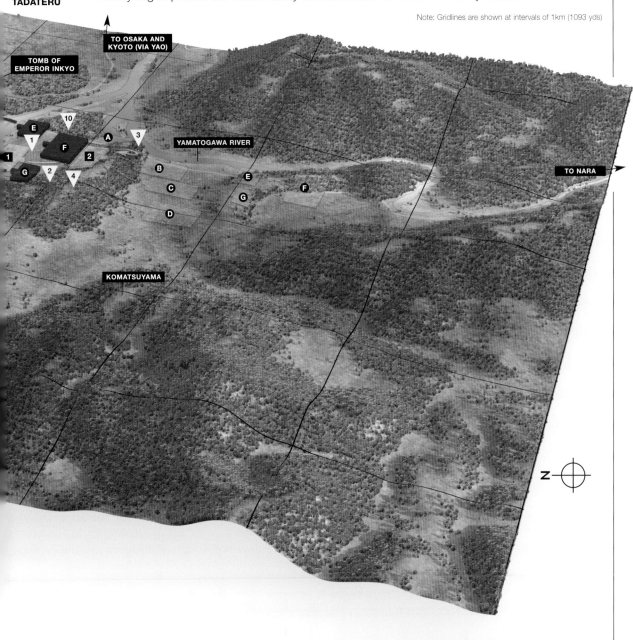

The strangest memento of the Summer campaign of Osaka is the 'bloody ceiling' of the Jokoji Temple in Yao. Todo Takatora held the traditional head-viewing ceremony inside the temple. The blood that seeped from the heads stained the floorboards, and this floor is now preserved as the ceiling of the Jokoji.

Tadamasa and Matsudaira Tadaaki back down the paths, but many more Tokugawa were approaching, including a particularly large contingent of 10,000 under Date Masamune. Numbers began to tell, but Mototsugu was determined to make a stand on top of Komatsuyama until the rest of the Osaka army arrived. At about 10.00am, while the Osaka main body was still blundering through the fog, Goto Mototsugu was shot and committed *seppuku*.

The Tokugawa army pressed on – some coming down the hill, others simply continuing along the road towards Domyoji. By now the fog had cleared, and the Osaka army was revealed on the opposite bank of the Ishikawa. The Tokugawa side crossed the river to meet them in battle beside the imperial tombs. Leading the left wing of the Osaka army was Susukida Kanesuke. He was still in disgrace from having been in a brothel while his fort was being captured, and he was determined to redeem himself. He was killed in action at Domyoji and was buried on the battlefield, where his grave is still cared for.

Fierce fighting continued, but as the Osaka side had already lost two outstanding generals in the action, Sanada Yukimura did not dare lose more, so he ordered a retreat to the castle. The Tokugawa army was as exhausted as he was, and the freshest of its contingent – that commanded by Ieyasu's sixth son Tokugawa Tadateru – was ordered to lead the pursuit. But Tadateru had had a long march, and refused to obey. It was an act of insubordination that was to cost him dear. In the event the Osaka army withdrew in fairly good order, unlike their comrades not far to the north, who were making another desperate attempt to hinder the inexorable advance of the Tokugawa.

The battle of Yao: 3 June 1615

The villages of Wakae and Yao, which are now suburbs of Greater Osaka, were then tiny hamlets in the middle of rice fields. The Ikoma range lay in the distance, and with no *kofun* around the whole area was very flat. It was also criss-crossed by a number of rivers and streams that fed the Osaka estuary. Several key roads leading to Osaka from the passes in the Ikoma mountains ran across the area. The Tokugawa advance, however, was not coming over the passes; Ieyasu had decided not to risk the superstition about Kuragari. Instead the advance was following the southern road, ready to split up off various points and head west towards the castle.

It was at its southern end that the first collision occurred. Here Chosokabe Morichika with 5,300 men attempted to stop the advance by Todo Takatora's 5,000 samurai near to the village of Yao. In this he was unsuccessful, but the fighting deprived Takatora of his two sons Takanori and Ujikatsu. They are buried in the grounds of the Jokoji Temple in Yao, where a very unusual memento of the battle has been preserved. Todo Takatora held the traditional head-viewing ceremony inside the temple, and there was not enough time to perform the ritual according to the preferred procedure. This would have involved the heads being washed, labelled with the name of the deceased and his vanquisher, having cosmetics applied and the hair combed, and the whole presented on a spiked wooden board. Instead the heads of the slain were brought before Todo Takatora in a somewhat freshly gathered condition. The blood that seeped from them stained the floorboards, and this floor is now preserved as the ceiling of the Jokoji.

The battle of Wakae: 3 June 1615

While the battle of Yao was being fought, a further action was taking place near the village of Wakae. Here Kimura Shigenari, ably assisted by Naito Sadatori and Yamaguchi Hirosada, attempted to stop another movement by a division of the Tokugawa army. He may have hoped to catch Tokugawa Ieyasu, who was known to be heading in that direction, but instead he ran into Ii Naotaka and his 'red devils'. The battle is depicted on one of Japan's finest painted battle screens, which is in Hikone Castle Museum; it shows the red devils in action, the samurai charging along with their red *sashimono* bearing their names flapping in the wind. Beginning with a volley from their arquebusiers, the Ii under Naotaka charged forward with allied units on their flanks. Having fired their arquebuses the *ashigaru* gunners shouldered their weapons and ran along beside the bulk of the cavalry and the large number of foot soldiers carrying the red banners. The Kimura samurai were soon in full retreat. Kimura Shigenari was killed and his head cut off, and several of the Ii samurai claimed the credit for such an illustrious prize. The head was finally taken to Tokugawa Ieyasu by Ando Shigekatsu (1597–1623), whose 'red devil' armour is kept by Osaka Castle Museum. Ieyasu, who always appreciated a good head when he saw one, presented Shigekatsu with five gold coins as a reward, and noted that Kimura Shigenari had burned incense inside his helmet prior to the battle in order to make his severed head a more attractive trophy. Ieyasu commended the practice to his followers. Shigenari is buried on the battlefield, where a statue of him has been erected.

Kimura Shigenari's brother Muneaki detached himself from the disaster of Wakae and, with only 300 men, headed north to the village of Yoshida, where a huge Tokugawa force was advancing. They were the advance troops of the main body that contained Ieyasu and Hidetada. The army included Sakakibara Yasukatsu and Ogasawara Hidemasa. Neither of these two *daimyo* went into action, because the Tokugawa vanguard under Niwa Nagashige simply brushed Muneaki aside.

There was no more hindrance in the way of the Tokugawa army. Ieyasu suggested to Hidetada that they should take up their former positions on Chausuyama and Okayama and begin the siege, but a surprise was in store for them: in spite of the expanse of wasteland and rubble that marked the site of what had once been the southern wall and the Sanada maru, the two hills were already occupied by a massive army of desperate men. The last samurai battle was about to begin.

THE BATTLE OF TENNOJI

A council of war was held inside Osaka Castle on the evening of 3 June. Toyotomi Hideyori must have looked in horror at the empty spaces where some of his best advisers had once sat. Those who had been spared during their brave attempt to stop the Tokugawa gave their opinion, and the decision was made. They could not risk a siege of Osaka Castle. Instead a battle would be fought on the fields to the south between the Hiranogawa and the sea.

Japanese historians have sometimes described the battle of Tennoji as if it were two separate actions fought on the flanks and converging in the

Todo Takatora's equestrian statue in the courtyard of Imabari Castle.

Kimura Shigenari, as depicted on a statue of him on the site of his command post at the battle of Wakae.

THE SUMMER CAMPAIGN: THE BATTLE OF TENNOJI, 4 JUNE 1615

The first phase: the battle of Tennojiguchi, showing the initial positions of the Eastern army at 12.00pm.

Note: Gridlines are shown at 1km (1093yds). Hill heights are given in brackets and are measured in metres.

OSAKA ARMY
1 Akashi Morishige
2 Ehara Takatsugu
3 Yoshida Yoshikore
4 Kimura Muneaki
5 Asai Nagafusa
6 Takeda Eio
7 Mori Katsunaga
8 *ronin*
9 Sanada Yukimura

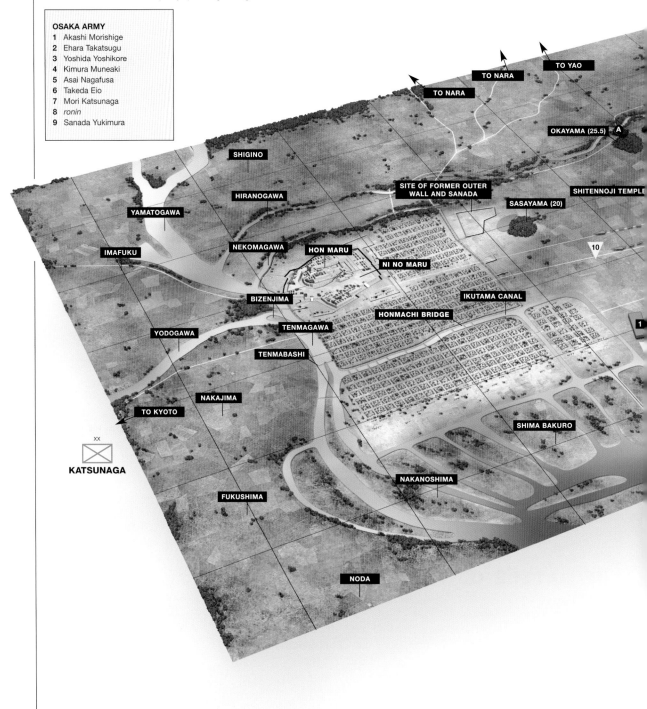

TO NARA

TO YAO

TO NARA

OKAYAMA (25.5)   A

SHIGINO

SITE OF FORMER OUTER WALL AND SANADA

SHITENNOJI TEMPLE

HIRANOGAWA

SASAYAMA (20)

YAMATOGAWA

10

NEKOMAGAWA

HON MARU

NI NO MARU

IMAFUKU

IKUTAMA CANAL

BIZENJIMA

HONMACHI BRIDGE

YODOGAWA

TENMAGAWA

TENMABASHI

NAKAJIMA

SHIMA BAKURO

TO KYOTO

XX
KATSUNAGA

FUKUSHIMA

NAKANOSHIMA

NODA

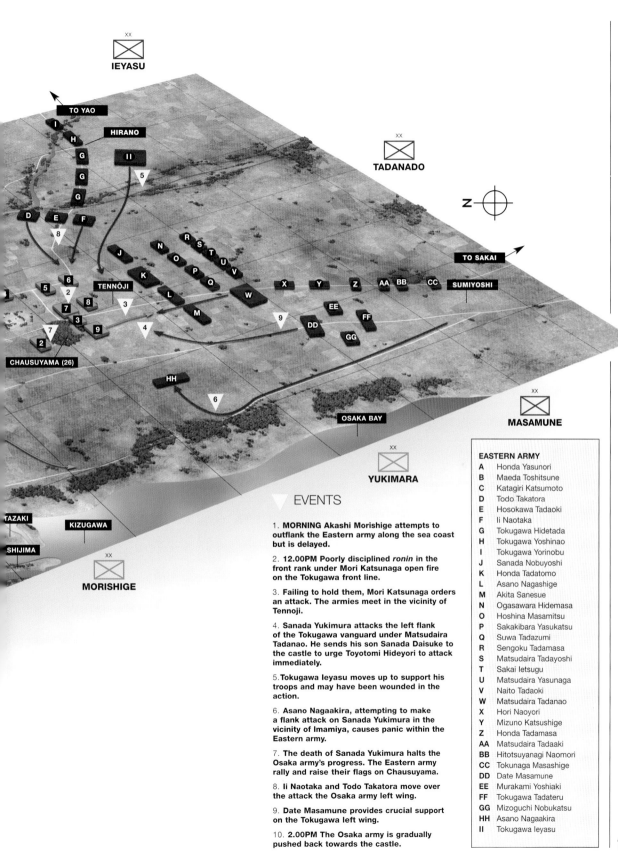

IEYASU

TO YAO

HIRANO

II

TADANADO

TO SAKAI

TENNŌJI

SUMIYOSHI

CHAUSUYAMA (26)

HH

OSAKA BAY

MASAMUNE

TAZAKI

KIZUGAWA

SHIJIMA

YUKIMARA

MORISHIGE

EVENTS

1. **MORNING** Akashi Morishige attempts to outflank the Eastern army along the sea coast but is delayed.

2. **12.00PM** Poorly disciplined *ronin* in the front rank under Mori Katsunaga open fire on the Tokugawa front line.

3. **Failing to hold them, Mori Katsunaga orders an attack. The armies meet in the vicinity of Tennoji.**

4. **Sanada Yukimura attacks the left flank of the Tokugawa vanguard under Matsudaira Tadanao. He sends his son Sanada Daisuke to the castle to urge Toyotomi Hideyori to attack immediately.**

5. **Tokugawa Ieyasu moves up to support his troops and may have been wounded in the action.**

6. **Asano Nagaakira, attempting to make a flank attack on Sanada Yukimura in the vicinity of Imamiya, causes panic within the Eastern army.**

7. **The death of Sanada Yukimura halts the Osaka army's progress. The Eastern army rally and raise their flags on Chausuyama.**

8. **Ii Naotaka and Todo Takatora move over the attack the Osaka army left wing.**

9. **Date Masamune provides crucial support on the Tokugawa left wing.**

10. **2.00PM** The Osaka army is gradually pushed back towards the castle.

EASTERN ARMY	
A	Honda Yasunori
B	Maeda Toshitsune
C	Katagiri Katsumoto
D	Todo Takatora
E	Hosokawa Tadaoki
F	Ii Naotaka
G	Tokugawa Hidetada
H	Tokugawa Yoshinao
I	Tokugawa Yorinobu
J	Sanada Nobuyoshi
K	Honda Tadatomo
L	Asano Nagashige
M	Akita Sanesue
N	Ogasawara Hidemasa
O	Hoshina Masamitsu
P	Sakakibara Yasukatsu
Q	Suwa Tadazumi
R	Sengoku Tadamasa
S	Matsudaira Tadayoshi
T	Sakai Ietsugu
U	Matsudaira Yasunaga
V	Naito Tadaoki
W	Matsudaira Tadanao
X	Hori Naoyori
Y	Mizuno Katsushige
Z	Honda Tadamasa
AA	Matsudaira Tadaaki
BB	Hitotsuyanagi Naomori
CC	Tokunaga Masashige
DD	Date Masamune
EE	Murakami Yoshiaki
FF	Tokugawa Tadateru
GG	Mizoguchi Nobukatsu
HH	Asano Nagaakira
II	Tokugawa Ieyasu

The death of Kimura Shigenari at the battle of Wakae. While an attendant holds his *sashimono*, one of the Ii 'red devils' joins his two comrades in making an end of the Osaka army's fine young general. From a painted screen in Hikone Castle Museum.

Sanada Yukimura in action during the battle of Tennojiguchi.

middle. It is a model that provides a convenient means for examining this most complex of battles, and will be adopted here.

Taking up positions: 12.00pm, 4 June 1615

The reason that Tokugawa Ieyasu was unable to take up his old position on Chausuyama was that the eminence was now occupied by the de facto commander of the Osaka army: Sanada Yukimura. As there was no fog to hide anyone's movements, the sight must have been breathtaking. To Yukimura's left stood the troops of Kimura Muneaki, who had fought at Wakae, and a large contingent under the command of Mori Katsunaga, whose own troops were augmented by many *ronin*. Approaching them from the south along the road from the Sumiyoshi Shrine came detachments under Sanada Nobuyoshi, soon to come face to face with his brother, followed by Honda Tadatomo, Asano Nagashige and Akita Sanesue. These four *daimyo* made up the vanguard on Ieyasu's left flank. Behind them were Ogawasara Hidemasa, Hoshina Masamitsu, Sakakibara Yasukatsu, Suwa Tadazumi and Ieyasu's grandson Matsudaira Tadanao, who had fought capably at the Hachomeguchi action in the winter. Date Masamune held the road that lay parallel towards the seacoast, while behind him stood Asano Nagaakira of Wakayama, whose movements in the next few hours were to prove crucial.

Out on the right wing of the Tokugawa army there was still considerable movement. With the large army of Maeda Toshitsune, flanked by Katagiri Katsumoto and Honda Yasunori as his vanguard, Tokugawa Hidetada was approaching Osaka from Hirano, keeping close to the Hiranogawa on his right for protection. Behind him came his nephews Tokugawa Yorinobu and the newly wed Tokugawa Yoshinao, eager for their first taste of battle. On his left were the reliable contingents under Todo Takatora, Hosokawa Tadaoki and Ii Naotaka. Hidetada's target was the high ground at Okayama. Ieyasu was somewhat to the rear, but heading for Chausuyama. The Osaka army on this flank was nowhere near at that point, but was proceeding steadily from the area of the former Sanada maru.

The Osaka side had a plan, and it was a good one. They knew they were heavily outnumbered. Fifty-four thousand is a good approximation of their total number, which is impossible to calculate accurately owing to the rapid and haphazard arrival of *ronin*. Sanada Yukimura and Mori Katsunaga would hold the Tokugawa in the centre of their 150,000-odd force. Meanwhile Akashi Morishige would make a wide sweep out to the right along the seacoast, and fall on Ieyasu's army from the side. Chosokabe Morichika would watch for an opportunity to make a similar assault onto the Tokugawa right flank. At this point Toyotomi Hideyori would sally out of Osaka Castle, bearing aloft his father's golden gourd standard.

The battle of Tennojiguchi: 12.00pm, 4 June 1615

It was indeed a good plan, particularly as the main body of the Tokugawa army was still strung out along the roads, having made a prudent sweep round from the Yao and Wakae areas. But the timing was crucial. The Osaka soldiers could not attack too late and thereby let the Tokugawa take up ordered positions. But neither could they attack too soon, and unfortunately for them, their position on Chausuyama on their right flank was just a little too secure. There they sat, and the left wing of the Tokugawa sat too, having dressed ranks long before the majority of their comrades. Sitting and waiting was not conducive to the spirit of the samurai. It was even less conducive to the spirit of the *ronin*, and there were a good many of these characters – ragged, desperate, vengeful and undisciplined – right in front of the Tokugawa vanguard.

The first shots of the last samurai battle were fired by these *ronin*. No order had been given either by their commander Mori Katsunaga or their supreme commander Sanada Yukimura, who had the best view of what was going on. When ordered to stop firing by these two eminent leaders the *ronin* simply ignored them and carried on at twice the rate of fire. Akashi Morishige was nowhere in sight. In fact he had succeeded in becoming lost – a remarkable achievement on a summer's day by the sea. Being unable to control his men, Mori Katsunaga surrendered himself to their adrenalin and ordered a general advance. Dividing his

The red lacquered armour of Ando Shigekatsu of the Ii 'red devils', who took Kimura Shigenari's head to Ieyasu, and received a reward of gold coins.

The site of the death of Sanada Yukimura is marked by the Yasui Shrine, which is located west of the Shitennoji Temple.

THE SUMMER CAMPAIGN: THE BATTLE OF TENNOJI, 4 JUNE 1615

The second phase: the Battle of Okayamaguchi and the fall of Osaka Castle.

Note: Gridlines are shown at 1km (1093yds). Hill heights are given in brackets and are measured in metres.

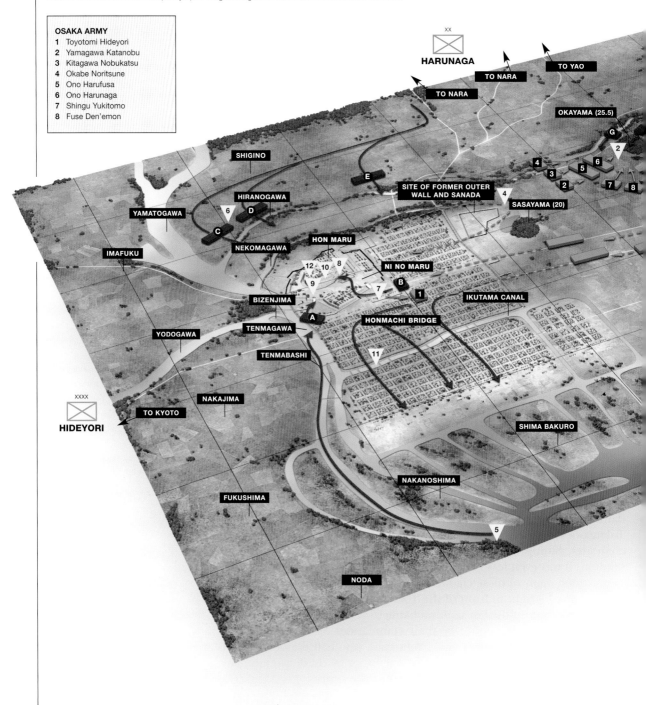

OSAKA ARMY
1. Toyotomi Hideyori
2. Yamagawa Katanobu
3. Kitagawa Nobukatsu
4. Okabe Noritsune
5. Ono Harufusa
6. Ono Harunaga
7. Shingu Yukitomo
8. Fuse Den'emon

XX
HARUNAGA

TO NARA

TO YAO

TO NARA

OKAYAMA (25.5)

SHIGINO

E

SITE OF FORMER OUTER
WALL AND SANADA

HIRANOGAWA

SASAYAMA (20)

YAMATOGAWA

D

6

C

NEKOMAGAWA

HON MARU

IMAFUKU

12 10 8

NI NO MARU

9

7   B

BIZENJIMA

1

A

IKUTAMA CANAL

TENMAGAWA

HONMACHI BRIDGE

YODOGAWA

TENMABASHI

11

NAKAJIMA

XXXX

TO KYOTO

HIDEYORI

SHIMA BAKURO

NAKANOSHIMA

FUKUSHIMA

5

NODA

78

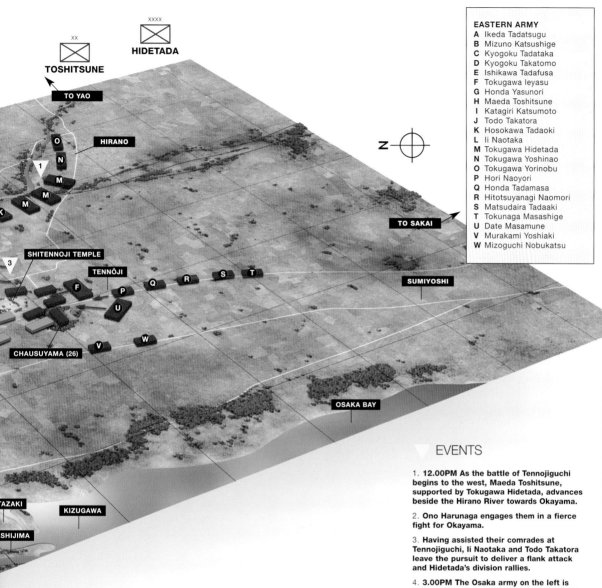

TOSHITSUNE

HIDETADA

TO YAO

HIRANO

O

N

M

1

M

M

K

M

Z

SHITENNOJI TEMPLE

3

TENNŌJI

F

P

Q

R

S

T

U

SUMIYOSHI

V

W

CHAUSUYAMA (26)

TO SAKAI

TAZAKI

KIZUGAWA

OSAKA BAY

ASHIJIMA

EASTERN ARMY
A Ikeda Tadatsugu
B Mizuno Katsushige
C Kyogoku Tadataka
D Kyogoku Takatomo
E Ishikawa Tadafusa
F Tokugawa Ieyasu
G Honda Yasunori
H Maeda Toshitsune
I Katagiri Katsumoto
J Todo Takatora
K Hosokawa Tadaoki
L Ii Naotaka
M Tokugawa Hidetada
N Tokugawa Yoshinao
O Tokugawa Yorinobu
P Hori Naoyori
Q Honda Tadamasa
R Hitotsuyanagi Naomori
S Matsudaira Tadaaki
T Tokunaga Masashige
U Date Masamune
V Murakami Yoshiaki
W Mizoguchi Nobukatsu

▼ EVENTS

1. **12.00PM As the battle of Tennojiguchi begins to the west, Maeda Toshitsune, supported by Tokugawa Hidetada, advances beside the Hirano River towards Okayama.**

2. **Ono Harunaga engages them in a fierce fight for Okayama.**

3. **Having assisted their comrades at Tennojiguchi, Ii Naotaka and Todo Takatora leave the pursuit to deliver a flank attack and Hidetada's division rallies.**

4. **3.00PM The Osaka army on the left is driven back towards the fortress along with the retreating right wing from Tennojiguchi.**

5. **Ikeda Tadatsugu, arriving by sea, secures Nakanoshima and attacks Osaka Castle from the Tenma River.**

6. **Ishikawa Tadafusa, Kyogoku Tadataka and Kyogoku Takatomo complete a flanking move and attack the castle from the northeast.**

7. **Toyotomi Hideyori leads an advance out of the castle, but only proceeds a short distance beyond the walls before retiring.**

8. **4.00PM Leading the Tokugawa advance, Mizuno Katsushige plants his standard at the Sakura gate.**

9. **The Tokugawa artillery fire on the keep**

10. **5.00PM: Osaka Castle is mysteriously set on fire.**

11. **The Tokugawa army engage the Osaka army in hand to hand fighting in the streets of the castle town as civilians flee in terror.**

12. **MORNING, 5 JUNE: Toyotomi Hideyori commits suicide.**

Samurai in action during the Summer campaign, as shown in this lively model spear fight in the permanent exhibition about the siege of Osaka in Osaka Castle Museum.

Tokugawa Ieyasu in command during the Summer campaign. He is surrounded by his messengers, who wear the distinctive 'go' character on their *sashimono*.

unit roughly into two, they fell upon the Tokugawa vanguard, who were scattered by the attack, and withdrew in disorder into the face of Matsudaira Tadanao's large contingent behind them. These men soon received an attack of their own from Sanada Yukimura, who descended from Chausuyama and assaulted them in the flank. Fearing that his fine plans would be ruined, Yukimura sent his son Sanada Daisuke at a gallop towards Osaka Castle, to urge Toyotomi Hideyori to make his grand entrance very quickly indeed.

At that point things became much worse for the Tokugawa side. Sanada Yukimura and Mori Katsunaga were already driving them back when there was an unexpected development. Asano Nagaakira of Wakayama had been moving round the extreme left flank of the Tokugawa army with the intention of making a flank attack on the Osaka side somewhere near Imamiya. But when he moved in for his attack he found that he had misjudged his distance and was advancing by mistake against the left flank of the Tokugawa army, not their enemies. Memories were evoked of Sekigahara, a battle that had been won for the Tokugawa by a defection and a treacherous attack. Cries of 'Treason!' went up, and something like panic ensued in the next few minutes.

Matters were so serious for the Tokugawa army that Ieyasu, who had been heading in the direction of the attack, hurried over to steady his troops. He was obviously very concerned, because we are told that he watched from beside the road accompanied by only one attendant. It is at this point that the strangest story of the whole Osaka campaign is told. Sanada Yukimura, advancing at the head of his victorious samurai, saw Tokugawa Ieyasu virtually unprotected, and engaged him in single combat. One version of the story has Ieyasu wounded by a spear thrust to his kidneys. The other, outrageous version, tells us that Tokugawa Ieyasu was killed. His place on the battlefield was immediately taken by a *kagemusha* (double), so that his men would not lose heart. If anyone doubts this story, say the Toyotomi conspiracy theorists, then he must betake himself to the Nanshoji Temple in Sakai, where Tokugawa Ieyasu is buried. His name is on the gravestone, just to prove it. As for the glorious Toshogo Shrine in Nikko, that holds nothing but the body of the *kagemusha*.

If Tokugawa Ieyasu had been killed in that encounter, and there is no evidence to suggest that he was, then the Tokugawa were much more successful at recovering from it than were the Osaka army a few minutes later. Because at that point Sanada Yukimura – and without question it was the real Sanada Yukimura – was killed. This tragic event, which happened in the open and with many witnesses, occurred when Yukimura, too tired to fight on, collapsed exhausted on a camp stool. A certain Nishio Nizaemon recognized him. Yukimura confirmed his identity, and took off his helmet. Nizaemon lopped off Yukimura's head, and rode off in triumph with the crucial trophy.

The Osaka army, bereft of its leader, began to give way under the pressure of a fresh attack by Ii Naotaka and Todo Takatora, whom Hidetada had sent over from his side of the battle. They succeeded in tipping the balance in favour of the Tokugawa and then withdrew to assist Hidetada, although not without loss, particularly among Todo Takatora's division, who had the unpleasant experience of having a land mine exploded among them. Finally, the 'one-eyed dragon' Date Masamune, who had hardly moved since the start of the battle of Tennojiguchi, advanced into action, coldly firing on one of his own men who was resting after an attack, on the grounds that his conduct looked suspicious. The Osaka army began to fall back towards the castle, and in the vicinity of the former Sanada maru it encountered some of its comrades who were doing precisely the same thing from the direction of Okayamaguchi. To explain what had been happening over on the other side of the field, we must turn to the parallel battle of Okayamaguchi.

The battle of Okayamaguchi: 12.00pm, 4 June 1615

Tokugawa Hidetada, at the head of a long crocodile of Tokugawa household troops, had been following his vanguard towards Okayama when the fighting erupted over towards the west. On his flank the battle of Okayamaguchi, a contest to gain the modest hill of Okayama, was fought between Maeda Toshitsune and Ono Harunaga. It

The most bizarre site connected with the siege of Osaka is within the courtyard of the Nanshoji Temple in Sakai. This, according to a persistent tradition, is the grave of Tokugawa Ieyasu, who was said to be killed during the Summer campaign. To avoid panic, his place was taken by a double.

Date Masamune in action during the battle of Tennoji, from the painted screen of the Summer campaign.

**TOYOTOMI HIDEYORI PREPARES TO LEAVE OSAKA CASTLE
FOR THE LAST TIME, 4 JUNE 1615** (pages 82–83)

The Tokugawa samurai are approaching the inner defences
of Osaka Castle, and Toyotomi Hideyori has finally decided
to ride out and do battle with the enemy. He has climbed
on to one of the wooden observation platforms inside the
castle so that he may address his men (1). As he is about
to set off on his last battle, I have used artistic licence and
chosen to dress him appropriately, so he is wearing his
late father Toyotomi Hideyoshi's sunburst helmet (2) and
jinbaori (surcoat) which is elaborately embroidered (3).
He also brandishes father's pearl-encrusted war fan to
encourage his men (4). Beside him stands Sanada Daisuke,
whose father Yukimura has just been killed, although he
does not know it. Daisuke is wearing the suit of armour in

which he is depicted on the Osaka screen (5). In the
courtyard are gathered a mixture of Hideyori's personal
retainers and many *ronin* all united in their determination
to curtail the Tokugawa advance in one desperate charge.
Casks of *sake* (6) are broken open and distributed among
the men, one of whom brandishes Hideyoshi's golden
gourd standard (7). On the wall is the *furanki* cannon
known as 'Taro', wedged into a solid wood block (8).
The flags of Hideyori's allies fly proudly. We see from left
to right the black and white bands of Mori Katsunaga (9),
the gold banners of Hideyori's direct retainers (10), the gold
mountain of Aoki Nobushige (11), the coin motif of Sanada
Daisuke (12), the red and white flag of Sano Yorizutsu (13),
the crosses of Akashi Teruzumi (14) and the black discs on
yellow of Chosokabe Morichika (15). All are ready to give
their lives in a final effort. (Richard Hook)

The townspeople flee in terror as Osaka Castle falls to the Tokugawa. This detail from the painted screen of the Summer campaign in Osaka Castle Museum shows the Tokugawa troops spreading out from the castle into the area of the castle town to the west of the keep.

The defence of a gateway into Osaka Castle at the conclusion of the Summer campaign. From a painted screen depicting the siege of Osaka in the Hosei Niko Memorial Museum, Nagoya.

was a ferocious battle, and threatened to go against the Tokugawa. Ii Naotaka and Todo Takatora hurried back to provide support, but so fierce was the fire that both of the Ii standard bearers were killed. The Ii ninja unit under Miura Yo'emon fought alongside the regular troops, and as evidence of their success a record states:

Item, one head: Miura Yo'emon
In the same unit:
Item, two heads: Shimotani Sanzo
Item, one head: Okuda Kasa'emon
Item, one head: Saga Kita'emon.

The suicide of Yodogimi, Hideyoshi's widow and the mother of Hideyori. She was very influential in accepting the peace agreement that ended the Winter campaign.

As the battle raged Tokugawa Hidetada was all for throwing himself into the fight, and had to be restrained from so doing by his bodyguard, who seized his horse's bridle. But Hidetada managed to hold his line, and just as the Osaka troops were beginning to be forced back from Tennojiguchi, a similar operation began on the Tokugawa right flank.

The operation very soon developed into one of pursuing the retreating Osaka army back to the castle. The process was helped by two flank attacks that actually succeeded in their aims. The first was launched by Ikeda Tadatsugu, who arrived by sea, secured Nakanoshima and attacked Osaka Castle from the Tenma River. Meanwhile, Ishikawa Tadafusa, Kyogoku Tadataka and Kyogoku Takatomo completed an elaborate flanking move in the Shigino area and attacked the castle from the north-east.

It was about this time that Toyotomi Hideyori finally made an appearance. Rumours of treachery had abounded. If Hideyori left the castle, some said, then someone would set fire to it, and by the time Sanada Daisuke persuaded him to ride out it was already too late. The painted screen of the Summer campaign shows Hideyori somewhere beyond the inner bailey with his golden gourd standard, but he may have gone no further than the gate before he pulled back to take refuge. By now the Tokugawa vanguard had reached the outer moat of the castle. At about 4.00pm in the afternoon the leader of the Tokugawa advance, Ieyasu's cousin Mizuno Katsushige (1546–1651), planted his standard at the Sakura gate.

THE FALL OF OSAKA CASTLE

Osaka Castle: 4.00pm, 4 June 1615

As the Tokugawa samurai surged towards the wet outer moats of Osaka Castle, Ieyasu's artillery began to open up on the keep once again. Seeing the hordes of *ronin* swarming in their direction, the townspeople of the *jokamachi*, who had led relatively settled lives since the end of the Winter campaign, began fleeing across the Ikutama Canal to the west.

A castle burns. Although this print does not depict Osaka, this must have been similar to the scene that met the eyes of the Tokugawa army on the night of their great victory. Note how the red sparks are leaping up into the air.

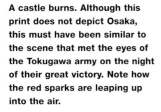

Many a scene of looting, violence and rape is portrayed on the second of the two painted screens in Osaka Castle Museum. Inside the Hon maru, meanwhile, there was a scene of utter chaos. Hideyori's household troops were succeeding in holding back the Tokugawa samurai from entering the Sakura gate, but inside the inner bailey the dire warnings about Hideyori leaving the castle had come true. Someone, believed to be Hideyori's chief cook, had set fire to the palace. A strong wind carried the flames far and wide, and by 5.00pm the inner moat had been breached under the cover of the smoke. Many of Hideyori's senior samurai committed *seppuku*. Ono Harufusa took refuge in flight, but other, cooler heads took control of the situation. Hideyori and Yodogimi sought refuge in the keep, to which the flames had not yet spread, but a senior councillor removed them to a fireproof storehouse. From there Ono Harunaga sent Sen hime, Hideyori's wife, under armed protection to seek sanctuary with her father Tokugawa Hidetada and her grandfather Tokugawa Ieyasu. She was indeed spared, and later married Honda Tadatoki. When she was widowed again she went to live near her brother, the third Tokugawa Shogun Iemitsu, and died in Edo at the age of 70.

The Hon maru of Osaka Castle: 5 June 1615

On the morning of 5 June Hideyori, in his fireproof refuge, not having received any favourable advances from Tokugawa Ieyasu and being shot at constantly by the Tokugawa artillery, decided to end it all. Some accounts say that he received orders to do so from Ieyasu himself. One of his retainers may have put an end to Yodogimi, although it is more likely that this proud lady took her own life in a way that befitted the consort of the great Hideyoshi. The 30 men and women who had accompanied them to their final refuge committed *seppuku*.

Okiku, the 20-year-old daughter of Yamaguchi Mozaemon, who was a lady-in-waiting to Yodogimi, provided a remarkable eyewitness account of the fall of Osaka Castle. She experienced the shock of seeing bullets hitting the kitchen tables: one tore the edge of a *tatami* (straw mat) and killed a maid. Okiku picked up one of the bullets in her palm. Yet she was so confident that Osaka would not fall that later on when she heard her maid shouting 'Fire!' she assumed that the girl was referring to the noodles she was cooking; actually the maid had spotted flames coming out of the Tamatsukuri gate of the castle. When the fire spread to the palace Okiku knew that she would have to evacuate the place. She put on three layers of clothing for fire protection and paused only to collect a mirror that Toyotomi Hideyori had once given her. Wounded soldiers called out for help as she passed. On escaping from the castle she met up with other women with whom she shared her extra kimono.

By now the fire had spread to the magnificent keep of Osaka Castle. No attempt was made to quench it, because all the energy of the Tokugawa army was now expended on pursuing the Osaka army. Most of its generals were now dead: either killed in battle or from suicide as the castle fell. Chosokabe Morichika was almost alone among the commanders in being captured and executed, but 72 lower-ranking officers were also beheaded and had their heads exposed. The same fate befell a huge number of *ronin*, who were summarily decapitated. The numbers must have been considerable, because the missionaries describe seeing their heads

Date Masamune was one of the veteran generals on the Tokugawa side during the Osaka campaign. This is a wax dummy of him at the Date Masamune Historical Museum in Matsushima. He is shown overcome by emotion as Osaka burns.

With the gourd standard of his late father behind him, Toyotomi Hideyori finally sallies out of Osaka Castle to do battle with the Tokugawa.

displayed on planks between Kyoto and Fushimi. There were 18 rows of planks, some with as many as 1,000 heads. The most pathetic victim of Ieyasu's purge, however, was Hideyori's son Kunimatsu, aged eight, who was found and beheaded in order not to leave an heir to the great Hideyoshi. In his diary of 12 June 1615 Richard Cocks notes:

> We had news today that Ogosho Samme [Ieyasu] hath taken the fortress
> of Osaka and overthrown the forces of Fidaia Samme [Hideyori]. Others
> say that most of the forces of Fidaia Samme issued out of the fortress,
> and sallied out 3 leagues toward Kyoto, but were encountered by the
> Emperor's forces and put to the worse, many of them being slaughtered
> and the rest driven back into the fortress.

A year later, when Cocks mentions Osaka in a letter to a trader elsewhere in East Asia, he is able to sum up the position as follows, with much emphasis, naturally, on what the Osaka campaign had done for business:

> Also we have had great troubles and wars in Japan since our arrival,
> which hath put us to much pains and charges in sending up and down
> to save our goods, and yet for all that some is lost and burned, two great
> cities being burned to the ground, each one of them being almost as big
> as London and not one house left standing, the one called Osaka and
> the other Sakai; and, as it is reported, above 300,000 men have lost
> their lives on the one part and other. Yet the old Emperour Ogosho
> Samme hath prevailed & Fidaia Samme either slain or fled secretly away
> that no news is to be heard of him.

A rumour that Hideyori was still alive continued for some time. Cocks writes on 28 September 1616 that:

> Capt. Adams went again to the Court to procure our dispatch, and
> found all the Council busied about matters of justice of life and death;
> and, amongst the rest, one man was brought in question about Fidaia
> Samme [Hideyori], as being in the castle with him to the last hour. This
> man was racked and tormented very much, to make him confess where
> his master was, or whether he were alive or dead; but I cannot hear
> whether he confessed any thing or no.

AFTERMATH

The end of the Summer campaign of Osaka marked the end of Japan's *Sengoku Jidai*, the Age of Warring States. It ushered in a period of two and a half centuries during which the Tokugawa family reigned supreme in a land that became almost totally cut off from the outside world by the inward-looking policies and paranoia of Ieyasu's successors. They may not have produced another Shogun to match Ieyasu, but his descendants were sufficiently competent to rule Japan until the threat from foreign nations in the 19th century made their position untenable, even though it was the Tokugawa Shogunate who were the progressives in establishing contact with the West.

Although the fall of Osaka Castle is now regarded as the decisive victory by the Tokugawa over their rivals, in the immediate aftermath Ieyasu's triumph was by no means so clear-cut. To the fears that Hideyori might have escaped were added concerns over trouble within the house of Tokugawa. In January 1616 Richard Cocks reported:

> *News is come the war is likely to ensue between the Emperor [Ieyasu]*
> *and his son Calsa sama [Tadateru] being backed by his father in law*
> *[Date] Masamune, because he will not give his son the fortress and*
> *territory of Osaka, if it were gotten, as he promised he would do.*

As Tokugawa Tadateru, Ieyasu's sixth son, had refused to pursue the Osaka army at the battle of Domyoji, this was an amazing claim to press, and his reward was to be exile to Koyasan. He eventually ended up in Suwa in Shinano province, where he died in 1683 at the age of 91.

With matters being so volatile the demand by the Tokugawa Shogun for European ordnance therefore continued, but unless ships simply sold their own cannon there was an unavoidably long time lag of up to two years between ordering weapons from Europe and actually receiving them. Shortly after the siege of Osaka a certain Jacques Specx, who had first arrived from the Netherlands in 1609, presented the Shogun with two iron sakers from the ship *Enchuijsen*, together with 100 roundshot and 350 *catties* of gunpowder. Specx then ordered to be cast in Hirado a gun of 273kg (600lb) weight, which was destined as a gift for 'Koshiki, president and chief counsellor of the old Emperor', in other words Honda Masazumi (1566–1637), Ieyasu's chief minister. Two more cannon were cast in Hirado on 6 August in order to replace the two sakers from the *Enchuijsen*, and Richard Cocks watched the proceedings:

> *Capt. Speck came late to the English house, and Sr. Matias with him,*
> *and desired my company to go and see a piece of ordnance cast which I*
> *did, but marvelled at their workmanship. For they carried the metal in*
> *ladles above 20 yards from the place where the mould stood, and so put*

Tokugawa Ieyasu, from a hanging scroll in the Nagashino Castle Memorial Hall.

it in, ladle after ladle, and yet made as formal ordnance as we do in Christendom, both of brass and iron. Capt. Speck told me neither workmanship nor stuff did not stand him in half the price it cost them in Christendom.

The East India Company also expressed concern over bad debts incurred by samurai who had the nerve to be killed at Osaka while owing them money. For example, the account books note that:

Previous to Aug 28 [1615] Watanabe Kuranosuke was directed to the factory at Osaka for broadcloth, coarse, 2 tatami [i.e. the cloth is measured against the area of a standard-sized Japanese straw mat], delivered unto him by Miguel the Korean, the interpreter, £26 0s 0d. Presently afterwards Watanabe Kuranosuke was slain in the wars, so this remains a desperate debt.

But what of the samurai who had not fought at Osaka? If a samurai was unable to demonstrate his martial prowess in battle, then the disgrace might be almost unbearable, although Shimazu Iehisa (1576–1638) does not seem to have suffered in this regard after arriving too late for the Winter campaign. However, a sad little anecdote in the chronicle *Meiryo Kohan* tells the story of a samurai who arrived too late to take part in the last great samurai battle that was the Osaka Summer campaign:

At the time of the siege of Osaka there was a man called Yabe Toranosuke, a retainer of Tokugawa Yorinobu of Kii province. He possessed great strength and had a three shaku tachi and for his sashimono he had a large ihai [mortuary tablet] on which was written the poem 'As there is no lack of flowers at blossom time,/So those defeated will not escape Yabe Toranosuke.' Many people watched his departure and all were amazed, but so many followed his horse as he advanced that it made him late, and in the end, to his regret, he was able to perform no meritorious deeds. Furthermore, his feelings were wounded by being insulted about the matter of his reputation by some within his family who were inexperienced in the martial arts, so he abstained from food for twenty days and thereby killed himself. This was extremely regrettable for a samurai.

As we now know, Yabe Toranosuke had indeed missed the final opportunity to take part in what the world would never see again: a pitched battle between two samurai armies. But it was almost three decades before the tension fully subsided. The uncertainty over whether or not the peace that Osaka had promised would last is noted by Cocks as late as 6 March 1622. In his diary he makes a comment upon further possible dissent within the Tokugawa family:

And, as I am informed, there will be wars shortly in Japan betwixt the Emperor and his uncle; for the Emperor sent to him to come and do his obeisance, as other subjects doe, or else he would take his revenues from him. But he returned answer he owed him no such service, and that if he went about to take his inheritance from him, he would defend it by arms. So that ten princes are sent to him to turn his mind, if not, then wars will ensue.

Wars did not in fact ensue. This affair came to nothing, and the only real threat to the Tokugawa emerged in 1638. The Shimabara Rebellion, which was to see some very fierce fighting, was a siege situation in which no spurious peace treaty could be negotiated, and turned out to be the only serious challenge to be mounted against the rule of the Tokugawa in two and a half centuries. The uprising, which had an important Christian element to it, began on the Amakusa islands and spread to the Shimabara peninsula to the south of Nagasaki. Having failed to capture the castle of Shimabara, the insurgents repaired the dilapidated castle of Hara that stood nearby, and held off the army of the Tokugawa for a period of several months.

Meanwhile Osaka Castle was rebuilt, and the city around it began to grow in a way that neither its founder Rennyo nor its most tragic inhabitant Toyotomi Hideyori could ever have dreamed of. The city had always housed a resilient merchant community, and as the years of the Tokugawa peace continued Osaka became renowned for the Bunraku puppet theatre, among other cultural delights. As its borders expanded with the dawn of the modern age, the centre of gravity shifted away from the castle and more to the north. The Nakajima area, the occupation of which by Ikeda Toshitaka had been the first gain by the Tokugawa in the Winter campaign, now houses Osaka Station, while Shin Osaka Station, on the route of the Shinkansen or 'Bullet Train', lies even further north across the re-routed Yodogawa. Yet Osaka Castle, an oasis of peace and greenery among the high-rise blocks of Japan's second metropolis, still has an air of being the true centre of the city. From its elevated position a feeling that this is the summit of a 'great slope' can still be discerned, and the massive stone walls that surround it still echo to the memories of the Winter and Summer campaigns.

Long before this time, however, all of the participants in Osaka 1615 had gone as guests to the White Jade Pavilion. Tokugawa Ieyasu departed this life in 1616. He brandished a sword on his deathbed and composed two farewell poems, as was fitting for Japan's greatest Shogun. After a short space of time his remains were interred in the magnificent Toshogo Shrine at Nikko, or, according to certain stubborn individuals, in the less than magnificent Nanshoji at Sakai.

Finally, in the year 1683, the man once known as Tokugawa Tadateru died in exile in the province of Shinano. Having fought during the battle of Domyoji and disobeyed orders, he had partly redeemed himself at Tennoji, only to lose everything when he opposed his father Ieyasu in 1616. For the rest of his life he was a wandering exile, until, as a 91-year-old monk whose previous identity was probably unknown to anyone around him, he finally went as a guest to the White Jade Pavilion. Thus died Tokugawa Tadateru, the man who was probably the final survivor of Japan's last samurai battle.

THE BATTLEFIELD TODAY

The events of the Osaka campaign took place over a very wide area, much of which has been swallowed up by the huge metropolitan area of modern Osaka. Yet much has been preserved, and as access is relatively easy Osaka provides one of the most rewarding Japanese battlefields to visit.

The starting point of any visit must be Osaka Castle. The keep is a ferro-concrete structure, but as it was based on the illustration of the building on the Osaka screen it is externally a very accurate reproduction of the keep that burned in 1615. Inside is one of Japan's best museums of military history. In keeping with Japan's museum policy of rotating collections, repeat visits will yield different objects, but as these include the original painted screens of the Osaka campaign and other battles, no visitor will ever be disappointed. One floor of the keep also has a permanent display about the Osaka campaign, with state-of-the-art audio-visual illustrations, sound effects, holograms and model soldiers. There is also a set of notices in English explaining the course of the Winter and Summer campaigns, and directions to places outside the castle where there are things to see. From the top floor the visitor can appreciate the dominant position of Osaka Castle, and receive a very good impression of the moats and the inner walls.

The walls and the moats marked on the map on page 34 as the 'south outer moat' etc are virtually unchanged from 1615, and present one of the classic examples of Japanese military architecture at its best. All of the modern Osaka Castle area is enclosed within this space. The gates and towers have been rebuilt, and the Oteguchi no longer leads to the temporary outer bailey, but to the main road beside the castle park. If this road is crossed one comes to the Osaka City Museum of History. As most of the displays about the castle are concentrated within the keep, this has very little about the campaigns, but has a splendid model of what the castle town of Osaka would have looked like at the time of Hideyoshi. The view of the castle from the windows is also superb.

A walk round the walls and the moat is recommended, because only then does one quite appreciate the sheer scale on which Osaka Castle was built. The size of the extra area that was temporarily enclosed during the Winter campaign is revealed by walking out of the Otemon and turning south. In ten minutes you will have reached the site of the Sanada maru, where there is a statue of Sanada Yukimura. Not far away is the site of Hidetada's headquarters on Okayama, now called Okachiyama, 'the mountain of victory'. Further walking, or a subway journey, leads to the site of the battle of Tennoji, which was fought around the area now occupied by Tennoji Station. To see the only open ground, a visit to the park is necessary, which includes Chausuyama. There is an admission fee, and an extra charge if you want to visit the zoo. Just to the north lies the Yasui Shrine, where Sanada Yukimura is buried. You can buy souvenir *ema* (prayer boards) with Yukimura's picture on. Interestingly, this is one of the best places in Osaka for appreciating the 'slope' on which the city is built.

The battle sites of the Summer campaign are easily visited using Osaka's extensive network of suburban trains. For Wakae go to the Kintetsu Namba Station and board the Kintetsu Railway bound for Nara via Fuse. Get off the train at Wakae Iwata, from where it is a short walk two blocks south to see the statue of Kimura Shigenari and his tomb. To visit Yao, get back on the train and go back as far as Fuse, then change lines for another outbound train, this time one heading for Yamato-Yagi. Alight at Kintetsu-Yao Station from which it is a very short walk to the Jokoji Temple, where the 'bloody ceiling' that was once the floor has been preserved. You can also see the graves of the members of the Todo family who were killed there.

Although not far away, Domyoji is approached by public transport via a different railway line, the Kintetsu Railway Minami Osaka Line from Tennoji. Ordinary express trains go straight through Domyoji without stopping, but this is to the visitor's advantage, because the next stop is Furuichi. Alight here and walk back about a mile towards Domyoji. The journey will take you across the battlefield, past the Konda Hachiman Shrine and the keyhole tomb of Emperor Ojin. Susukida Kanesuke's grave is in Domyoji, just beside the elevated motorway. Before getting on the stopping train at Domyoji to return to Osaka, you can take in the Ikoma hills and the river nearby. Incidentally, two stops down the line from Furuichi is Tondabayashi, the well-preserved 'temple town' of the Ikko-ikki.

The site of Kishiwada Castle and the battle of Kashii lie along the coast near to Kansai International Airport, while the final site on the Osaka battlefield is the strangest of all. This is the temple in Sakai called the Nanshoji, where the priest will be delighted to show you the grave of Tokugawa Ieyasu. A trip to Kyoto will be necessary to see the notorious temple bell. It still hangs in a tower, although the temple built to house it has long gone, and the successor to Hideyoshi's Great Buddha is a modern edifice that must be one of the ugliest statues in Japan. On the surface of the bell, picked out helpfully in white, is the insulting inscription that led to the last samurai battle.

Portrait of Tokugawa Ieyasu as the Shinto *kami* (deity) Tosho Daigongen ('The Great Incarnation Illuminating the East') in the Nikko Toshogo Museum.

The site of the battle of Wakae is now marked by this Shinto shrine where Kimura Shigenari is remembered.

BIBLIOGRAPHY

Various authors, *Osaka no jin*, Rekishi Gunzo Series 40, Tokyo (1994)

Various authors, *Sengoku Kassen Taizen*, Vol. 2 Rekishi Gunzo Series 51, Tokyo (1997)

Various authors, *Sanada Senki*, Rekishi Gunzo Series 7, Tokyo (1998)

Various authors, *Gekito: Osaka no jin*, Rekishi Gunzo Sengoku Selection, Tokyo (2000)

Various authors, *Senkyo Zuroku: Osaka no jin*, Rekishi Gunzo Yomihon 56 ,Tokyo (2003)

Boxer, C. R., *The Christian Century in Japan 1549–1650* Los Angeles (1951)

Boxer, C. R., *The Dutch Seaborne Empire 1600–1800* London (1965)

Bramsen, W., 'Japanese Chronological Tables' in *Transactions of the Asiatic Society of Japan* 37 (1910)

Farrington, A., *The English Factory in Japan 1613–1623 Volume 1*, London (1991)

Farrington, A., *The English Factory in Japan 1613–1623 Volume 2*, London (1991)

Lidin, O. G., *Tanegashima – The Arrival of Europeans in Japan*, Copenhagen (2002)

Massarella, D., *A World Elsewhere: Europe's Encounter with Japan in the Sixteenth and Seventeenth Centuries*, Yale (1990)

McClain, J. L. and O. Wakita, *Osaka: The Merchants' Capital of Early Modern Japan*, New York (1999)

Murakami, S. and K. Hozumi, *Osaka no jo*, Tokyo (1984)

Murdoch, J. H., *A History of Japan*, Volume 2, London (1951)

Sadler, A. L., *The Maker of Modern Japan: The Life of Tokugawa Ieyasu*, London (1937)

Sambo Hombu (General Staff HQ), *Osaka no jin (fuyu.natsu)*, Volume 7 of the series *Nihon no Senshi*, Tokyo (1965)

Sawada, H., *Sakai Zutsu*, Sakai (1982)

Thompson, E. M. (ed.), *Diary of Richard Cocks, Cape-merchant in the English Factory in Japan 1615–1622, with Correspondence*, Hakluyt Society 1st Series 66–67, London (1883)

Turnbull, S. R., *Japanese Fortified Temples and Monasteries AD 710–1602*, Osprey Fortress Series 34, Oxford (2005)

Yoshioka, S., *Collection of Antique Guns*, Tokyo (1965)

INDEX